PLANT-BASED Simple MADE

Simple. Nutritious. Delicious.

Teresa –
Thanks for always
being such a good
sport by tasting my creations.
(Even if it was chickpeas)!
Many Blessings and
Happy Cooking!
Carla
(3 John 2)

Wildwood
HEALTH INSTITUTE

Wildwood
HEALTH INSTITUTE

Wildwood Health Institute is a supporting ministry of the Seventh-day Adventist Church providing educational, health, business, and evangelistic services to our local and worldwide communities. Wildwood is a training hub and launch pad for the expansion of lifestyle centers, educational institutions, and city missions in and around major cities and rural areas all over the world for the salvation of souls. For more information, visit www.wildwoodhealth.org.

Wildwood
LIFESTYLE CENTER

From the very beginning, our philosophy at Wildwood Lifestyle Center has been to minister to individuals on all levels, reaching people exactly where they are. We care for them physically, mentally, and spiritually. At Wildwood, we believe in healing by changing lives, not just treating symptoms. Wildwood is a place where modern medicine meets nature's remedies and lifestyle change. At Wildwood Lifestyle Center, we don't just treat our guests during the program, but instead teach them everything they need to know, so that they can continue to live the healthy life that they have obtained during their stay. For more information, visit www.wildwoodhealth.com.

LIGHT

The Lay Institute for Global Health Training (LIGHT) is a supporting ministry of the Seventh-day Adventis church devoted to providing health evangelism training worldwide. For more information, visit to www.lightingtheworld.org.

DIY HEALTH

For plant-based cooking videos by Carin Lynch, and health and lifestyle tips, scan the QR code on the left for DIY Health on YouTube and the QR code on the right for Facebook.

First edition. Printed by College Press in Collegedale, TN, United States of America. Published by Wildwood Health Institute in Wildwood, GA, United States of America.

Dedicated to all those
who have chosen to
take their first steps
toward a healthier way
of eating. My prayer
is that this book will
create a pathway on
which you can start your
journey toward a more
abundant life.
- Carin

Table of *Contents*

Praise for Plant-Based Made Simple and Carin Lynch

"Plant-Based Made Simple isn't just another plant-based cookbook.
I encourage many of my patients to adopt a whole food plant-based diet, but the transition can be quite a challenge for some. Most recipes are either healthy but tasteless, or vegan junk food. Carin's cookbook paves the way for anyone, and I mean literally anyone, to become healthy without compromising flavor. I personally have enjoyed dozens of her dishes, and I can tell you that she has a gift for making healthy food taste great and keep you coming back for more!"

Tim Riesenberger, MD, MPH, FACEP
Alumnus of Loma Linda School of Medicine and former resident of Stanford Emergency Medicine

"Carin Lynch's enthusiasm at Wildwood Lifestyle Center's teaching kitchen has made lots of people excited about adopting a plant-based diet. Her new cookbook Plant-Based Made Simple will be like a whisk that many people will use to stir out old, poor eating habits and start afresh with recipes for a healthy body, mind, and soul."

Vaughan Sparrow
President of Wildwood Health Institute

> "Beloved, I pray that you may prosper in all things and be in health, just as your soul prospers."
>
> **3 JOHN 2**

SIMPLE, NUTRITIOUS, AND DELICIOUS

If you have ever been to one of my cooking classes, you have most definitely heard my catchphrase: "simple, nutritious, and delicious." It is the epitome of what quality food needs to be.

SIMPLE

Food should be easily made with simple ingredients. Cookbooks often contain long lists of food items that scare home cooks who want to put a meal on the table with little hassle. I have put together recipes that require just a few ingredients with simple preparation.

NUTRITIOUS

Isn't that the crux of the matter? God created whole foods for nutrition, perfectly packaged and balanced. Over the years we have modified, corrupted, and deconstructed God's perfect diet for mankind. However, we can go back to basics and retrain our tastebuds to desire nutritious food.

DELICIOUS

Last, but certainly not least, I've come to realize that the simplest and most nutritious foods mean nothing unless they taste good. I can assure you that if the food is not delicious, no one will eat it. Healthy food can taste great, I promise.

What I have strived to do is bring these three concepts together in one cookbook. I pray that as you take steps toward a healthier way of life, these recipes will be stepping stones to help you transition to a more whole food plant-based diet.

Carin

To schedule cooking or health evangelism classes, you can reach Carin Lynch at LIGHT (Lay Institute for Global Health Training) through ronandcarin@lightingtheworld.org, or by calling (706) 820-9804.

Carin
Wildwood

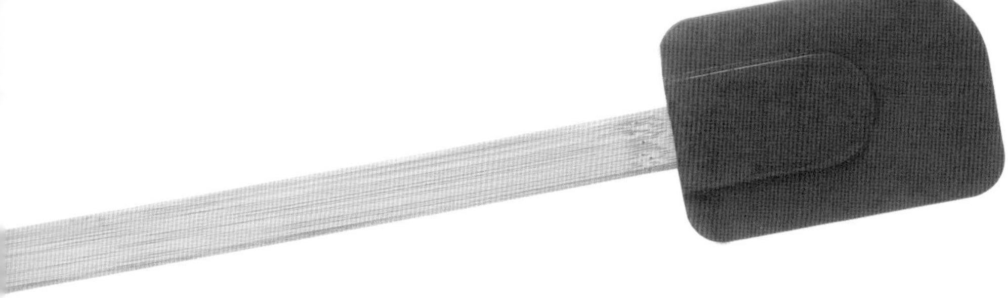

HOLD THAT SPATULA!

Some Need-to-Knows Before You Start Cooking

AGAR-AGAR

Agar-agar (sometimes referred to as just agar) is a vegetarian gelatin substitute made from seaweed. It is a substance that comes from red algae and becomes jelly-like when it's mixed with liquid and heated. It comes in a powder-form or flakes and can be found at health food stores or online. If you decide to use flakes instead of powder for my recipes, you have to triple the amount (so 1 tsp of powder would be 1 Tbsp of flakes).

AQUAFABA

Aquafaba is the liquid from canned or cooked chickpeas/garbanzo beans. It is a great substitute for eggs in baked goods, desserts, and most other recipes that call for eggs or egg whites. You can even freeze it to use at a later time.

BAKING POWDER

Throughout the years, there have been concerns about the use of baking powder or baking soda in recipes because of how it negatively affects the gastrointestinal system. Sodium bicarbonate, or baking soda, needs to be neutralized in order to be safe for consumption.

Baking powder specifically combines baking soda and an acid to create a leavening effect in baked goods. Are baking soda or baking powder safe to use? Many of the concerns that arose before the turn of the 20th century are no longer issues when it comes to using baking powder. In the 19th century, baking soda and food acid were packaged separately, and the home cook needed to combine the substances together to form baking powder. The problem was that it was almost impossible to accurately measure and safely balance the substances. Also, home cooks would often go heavy on the baking soda to make lighter and fluffier breads, cakes, and desserts.

Today, baking powder, especially aluminum-free brands, are completely neutralized and no longer present a risk. If you do need to use baking soda, a way to neutralize it is to add an acid. The ratio for acid to soda is 1 Tbsp of lemon juice for every 1/2 tsp of baking soda.

Personally, I try not to use baking soda in recipes. However, there are some recipes that need a bit of leavening, especially when using whole grains. When I come across these, I use baking powder which has already been neutralized. To play it safe, I sometimes add a little lemon juice just for good measure.

BRAGG COCONUT LIQUID AMINOS

Bragg Coconut Liquid Aminos is the soy-free version of Bragg Liquid Aminos. It is made from fermented coconut palm sap and salt. It is recommenced to eat fermented foods in moderation. Fermented foods may affect the gastrointestinal track, which can cause bloating and gassiness.

BRAGG LIQUID AMINOS

Bragg Liquid Aminos is a non-fermented, gluten-free soy sauce or tamari alternative. Soy sauce and tamari are both fermented which can irritate the stomach. Bragg is loaded with 16 amino acids which are the building blocks of protein. Use it in any recipe that calls for soy sauce or tamari.

BREAD CRUMBS

I've found that the easiest way to make great whole grain breadcrumbs is to save the ends of your bread loaves, bag them up, and pop them in the freezer until you are ready to use them. When needed, defrost and then process in a blender or food processor until you've reached the desired consistency. If you'd like, you can toast them before processing for a drier breadcrumb.

DEXTRINIZED BROWN RICE

Dextrinizing brown rice is a technique that not only makes your rice light and fluffy, but also makes it easier to digest. You can dextrinize it by toasting dry rice in a pan, without any oil or water, until it begins to brown and makes "popping" sounds. Then use the rice as usual in the recipe.

BUTLER SOY CURLS

Butler Soy Curls are a meat substitute that have a texture similar to chicken. Soy Curls are minimally processed and only contain non-GMO whole soybeans without any chemicals or preservatives. I break the Soy Curls into small pieces, then rehydrate them by adding chicken-like seasoning to a pot of water, enough to where it sits about an inch above the Curls. I then boil them for about 10 minutes. Lastly, I drain any excess water and use the Soy Curls like chicken in my recipes.

CAROB

Carob is a great substitute for chocolate without caffeine or dairy. Carob powder is made by drying, roasting, and then grinding the pods of a locust tree. Carob is full of calcium, magnesium, and potassium. In the Bible, John the Baptist had a diet of locust and wild honey in the wilderness. Looks like he had a bit of a sweet tooth. What do you think?

CHIA SEEDS

Chia seeds are rich in omega-3 fatty acids, protein, antioxidants, potassium, fiber, calcium, magnesium, and iron. They are a superfood that can easily be used as a binder in many recipes or baked goods. They are also delicious when sprinkled on cereal or other foods, and are fully digestible, so you don't need to grind them before eating.

COCONUT OIL

Coconut oil is a saturated fat, so limit your consumption to 2 to 3 Tbsps per week or less.

COCONUT SUGAR

Coconut sugar, which is a less processed sugar, is made from drying sap of the coconut palm. Compared to refined sugars, it is a lower glycemic food. Coconut sugar is less sweet to the taste than refined sugars, so using it is a way to retrain your taste buds to desire less sugary foods.

COFFEE SUBSTITUTES

Non-caffeinated herbal or roasted grain "coffee" products are a healthy substitute for regular coffee. Some examples to try are: Roma, Pero, Dandy Blend, Cafix, and Postum.

GRAINS OF PARADISE

Although not as pungent, Grains of Paradise is a substitute for black pepper. Indigenous to West Africa, the seasoning was a delicacy in Europe for many years. It is closely related to cardamom, giving its flavor a hint of citrus. As with any seasoning, use it sparingly.

HIMALAYAN PINK SALT

Himalayan pink salt is a great choice of salt for much of your cooking. Mined about 5,000 feet below sea level, it is 99% pure and has about 84 trace minerals. I try to stay away from sea salt because there is a risk of ingesting microplastics found in the salt. Regular table salt is probably the worst choice. It is stripped of all its minerals. Also, if it is iodized, it simply means that the manufacturers have added iodine after they've removed it. Table salt is overprocessed, containing added chemicals to make the salt easy to pour and not clump up.

KALA NAMAK

Kala namak, Himalayan black salt, or Indian black salt, is a rock salt used in South Asian cuisine. It has a sulfurous smell and tastes similar to a hard boiled egg. It adds the smell and flavor of eggs to plant-based dishes. You can find kala namak in Asian grocery stores or online.

KELP POWDER

Kelp powder comes from drying and grinding kelp, an algae seaweed. It is a great addition to plant-based foods, not only for its fishlike flavor, but also because it is a great source of iodine and many minerals, such as potassium, magnesium, calcium, and iron.

MAPLE SYRUP

When I talk about using maple syrup as a sweetener, I mean pure maple syrup, which is the all natural sap of the sugar maple tree. Don't be deceived by standard pancake syrup in the store, which doesn't contain maple syrup at all but artificial flavoring and high fructose corn syrup instead.

NUTRITIONAL YEAST FLAKES

Nutritional yeast is an active yeast that is grown on molasses. It is dried, heated to deactivate, and then ground. Nutritional yeast is used as an ingredient in many plant-based dishes. It has a delicious cheesy and nutty flavor, and is a great source of protein. Many varieties are fortified with B-vitamins, especially B12, which has been known to be deficient in many diets.

NUTS: TO SOAK OR NOT TO SOAK

Raw nuts, seeds, grains, and beans should be soaked for at least two hours and up to overnight. Not only does that make them easier to blend, but it also removes the enzyme phytic acid which can cause gassiness, some stomach discomfort, and possibly block the absorption of minerals in the small intestine, such as calcium, zinc, and iron.

OATS: GLUTEN-FREE OR NOT

Oats are a superfood. They are a great source of protein, soluble and insoluble fiber, and many vitamins and minerals. Oat groats are unprocessed. They are the healthiest type of oats you can eat. Steel cut oats are next in line. They are oat groats chopped up and minimally processed. They also contain more fiber than traditional rolled oats. What you'll usually find in the grocery store are rolled (old fashioned) oats and quick oats.

However, the question often arises: are oats gluten-free? Although oats do not naturally contain gluten, they are often processed in plants that mill gluten products, so the oats could be contaminated. If you are sensitive to gluten or have celiac disease, make sure to purchase gluten-free oats for any recipe that requires oats. Better safe than sorry.

OIL

Oil, as we know it, is a refined product. I try to use as little oil as possible in my recipes, but sometimes it is needed to get the right consistency, flavor, or texture. I use first cold pressed extra virgin olive oil almost exclusively in my dishes that require oil. It comes from a process in which the olives are pressed for the first time, without the use of heat. Olives are pressed a gazillion times to extract as much oil as possible. Heating the olives to a high temperature may increase the volume of oil, but also molecularly breaks down its composition, resulting in an unhealthy oil that could be a carcinogen.

QUINOA

Quinoa (pronounced "keenwa") is prepared as a grain, but is actually a seed and is a complete protein, having all of the essential amino acids. It also contains a good amount of calcium and phosphorus.

STEVIA

This is a healthy sugar substitute native to South America. It is virtually calorie- and carbohydrate-free because it is an herb and not an actual sugar. Look for the least processed brands. Be careful, Stevia is much sweeter than sugar, so use small amounts to start off with. It comes in leaf, powder, or liquid form.

TINKYADA BROWN RICE PASTA

Being an Italian-American, pasta was a staple food item in our house when I was a child. I still really enjoy a good plate of pasta, but most whole grain pastas just don't cut it for me. That's when I discovered pasta from the brand Tinkyada. It is a gluten-free whole grain brown rice pasta. Even though I am not gluten-free, I still like it a lot. The texture is great and the taste, in my opinion, is one of the best of the whole grain pastas on the market. You can find it in most health food stores and online. I've also occasionally seen it at Walmart.

TOFU

This food is a great source of protein that is often used in vegetarian and plant-based cooking. Studies have shown that tofu can help prevent heart disease and certain cancers. There are two varieties: silkened and regular packaged in water. Silkened tofu is smoother with a high water content. It is great for desserts, smoothies, and sauces. Regular tofu works best in savory dishes. I usually use firm or extra firm tofu, both when I use silkened or the regular kind. Tofu doesn't contain much flavor until you mix it with other ingredients or seasonings. It takes on the flavor of what it's being cooked with. Unfortunately, soy beans are about 92% genetically modified. Because of the health concerns with GMOs, purchase only organic or non-GMO tofu.

TURBINADO SUGAR

This is a less processed sugar, also known as sugar in the raw. It is a better choice than refined white sugar.

VANILLA

Vanilla flavoring is a processed food. A better option is to use natural vanilla bean. About two inches of vanilla bean equals one tsp of vanilla flavoring. Beware: vanilla bean is pricy but the flavor is incredible.

WRIGHT'S LIQUID SMOKE

Liquid smoke is a seasoning that gives food a wood smoke flavor similar to hickory or mesquite. I use Wright's Hickory Liquid Smoke because it does not contain vinegar, which is a known irritant to the mucous lining of the stomach.

HOW TO USE QR CODES

You'll notice that some recipes contain a QR code. Use your phone's camera app or QR code reader app and point it at the code to get a link to some of Wildwood's DIY Health YouTube videos with my recipes. In these videos I demonstrate how to make these dishes. Also, scan the code below for my welcome message to you. Happy cooking!

Breakfast

Chef Tips

For a lighter, less dense waffle, add 1 tsp aluminum-free baking powder. This will also reduce the cooking time.

CORN AND OAT WAFFLES

You'll Love Them a Waffle Lot

MAKES 4-5 LARGE ROUND WAFFLES
TOTAL TIME: 30 MINUTES OR LESS
GLUTEN-FREE | SOY-FREE | NUT-FREE (OPTIONAL) | OIL-FREE (OPTIONAL)

STUFF YOU NEED

3 1/4 cups oats
Use gluten-free oats if needed

4 cups water

3/4 cup grits or cornmeal

2 Tbsps extra virgin olive oil (or 1/4 cup nuts)

1 1/4 tsp Himalayan pink salt or salt of your choice

3 Tbsps honey, pure maple syrup, or raw blue agave nectar (or 1/4 cup dates, chopped and softened in warm water)

2 Tbsps vanilla or maple flavoring
See page 10 for the vanilla bean equivalent

LET'S COOK!

1. Preheat waffle iron.
2. Place all ingredients in a high speed blender and blend until smooth. This makes a thick waffle batter. If it's too thick, add a bit of water to thin the consistency to make a more pourable batter.
3. Cook waffles on a waffle iron until golden brown.

Chef Tips

I like to pour this fruit sauce on top of pancakes, waffles, or desserts.

For a smoother syrup, blend in a high speed blender until desired consistency is reached.

Since this makes a good-sized batch, freeze any leftovers for another time. To reheat, simply defrost overnight in the refrigerator and warm up in a pot on the stove. If needed, add water to get a smoother and more pourable batch.

FRUIT SAUCE
Very Berry Delicious

MAKES 5 CUPS
TOTAL TIME: 30 MINUTES OR LESS
GLUTEN-FREE | SOY-FREE | NUT-FREE | OIL-FREE

STUFF YOU NEED

5 cups fresh or frozen berries

1 1/2 cups water

1/2 cup raw blue agave nectar, honey, pure maple syrup, or 1 tsp stevia powder

1/3 cup cornstarch mixed with 1/2 cup water

LET'S COOK!

1. Bring berries, water, and sweetener to a boil.
2. Reduce heat to a simmer.
3. Add cornstarch to 1/2 cup water and mix until all lumps are gone.
4. Pour cornstarch mixture into berry mixture while stirring slowly.
5. Stir until topping thickens (about 1 to 2 minutes) and begins to bubble.

Chef Tips

For a crispy, raw, and nutritious granola, spread mixture on dehydrator trays and dehydrate for two days at 110°F (43°C). To keep it raw, eliminate dried fruit, unless you have dried them yourself below 118°F (48°C).

GRANOLA AND DESSERT TOPPING

For the 24/7 Sweet Tooth

MAKES 5 CUPS OF GRANOLA
GLUTEN-FREE (OPTIONAL) | SOY-FREE | OIL-FREE

STUFF YOU NEED

Dessert Topping
1/4 cup water

2 Tbsps pure maple syrup

1 tsp vanilla or maple flavoring
See page 10 for the vanilla bean equivalent.

1/4 tsp Himalayan pink salt or salt of your choice

1/2 cup dates, chopped and pitted (about 6)

1/3 cup walnuts

1/2 cup nuts, roughly chopped
Walnuts, pecans, almonds, etc.

3 cups old-fashioned oats
Use gluten-free oats if needed.

To Make Granola, Also Use the Following
1 cup old-fashioned oats
Use gluten-free oats if needed.

1 cup nuts, roughly chopped
Walnuts, pecans, almonds, etc.

1/2 cup dried fruit
Blueberries, cranberries, raisins, etc.

LET'S COOK!

1. Preheat oven to 200°F (93°C).

Dessert Topping

2. Put water, sweetener, flavoring, dates, and 1/3 cup of walnuts in a blender. Blend on high for about 1 minute until smooth.
3. Place chopped nuts and 4 cups of oats in a large mixing bowl. Allow mixture to cool.
4. Add blended mix to the oats and nuts and gently mix together with your hands.
5. If you are going to use it as a crumbly topping for a baked dessert, use this mixture raw to top fruit, and then bake for a delicious dessert.

Turn It Into Granola

6. To turn this into a granola, mix in an additional cup of oats and a cup of chopped nuts.
7. Place mixture loosely on a baking sheet or large jelly roll pan.
8. Bake in the oven for about 6 hours until toasty and golden brown.
9. Periodically turn granola to make sure that everything gets browned evenly.
10. When it's done, mix in dried fruit. Cool and store in an airtight container.

TEX-MEX TOFU SCRAMBLE

It Will Surpass Your "Eggspectation"

MAKES 4 TO 6 SERVINGS
TOTAL TIME: 30 MINUTES OR LESS
GLUTEN-FREE | NUT-FREE | OIL-FREE

STUFF YOU NEED

1 lb crumbled tofu

4 tsps of your favorite chicken-like seasoning
See recipe for Chicken-Like Seasoning on pages 178-179

1/2 tsp turmeric

1/2 tsp onion powder

2 tsps nutritional yeast flakes

1/4 to 1/2 tsp garlic powder

1/4 tsp Himalayan pink salt or salt of your choice

1/4 tsp kala namak (black salt)

1/2 cup onion, chopped

1/4 cup green pepper, chopped

2 to 4 Tbsps water

1/4 cup tomatoes, diced

4 scallions or green onions, sliced for garnish

Taco Seasoning to taste
See recipe on pages 180-181

LET'S COOK!

1. Rinse tofu in cold water and drain.
2. In a large mixing bowl, mash tofu into chunks with a fork or potato masher.
3. Mix in seasonings except Taco Seasoning.
4. In a skillet on medium-high heat, sauté onion and pepper in water until soft. You may need to add additional water to prevent the vegetables from sticking.
5. Add tofu mixture to skillet. Stir together on medium heat for 5 to 10 minutes.
6. When the consistency is like that of scrambled eggs, add diced tomatoes.
7. For a flavor boost, sprinkle a little bit of Taco Seasoning on top.
8. Garnish with scallions or green onions.

Chef Tips

This recipe makes the perfect stuffing for a breakfast burrito.

"UNSAUSAGE" PATTIES

No Meat, Period.

MAKES 10 PATTIES
GLUTEN-FREE | SOY-FREE (OPTIONAL)

STUFF YOU NEED

2 1/4 cups water

1/4 cup Bragg Liquid Aminos
Use Bragg Coconut Aminos for soy-free option

1 tsp garlic powder

1 1/2 tsps onion powder

1 1/2 Tbsps nutritonal yeast flakes

1 to 2 tsps dried sage

2 Tbsps extra virgin olive oil

2 Tbsps walnuts, ground

2 Tbsps sunflower seeds, ground

2 1/4 cups quick oats
Use gluten-free oats if needed

LET'S COOK!

1. Preheat oven to 375°F (191°C).
2. Place all ingredients except oats in a saucepan, and bring to a boil.
3. Add oats and cook for about 5 minutes, stirring constantly.
4. Allow mixture to cool.
5. Shape into patties and place on an oiled or non-stick baking sheet.
6. Bake for approximately 15 minutes on each side until lightly browned.

Chef Tips

To make uniform patties, use a small canning jar lid as a mold. (This is also great for portion control.) To prevent sticking, brush lid with extra virgin olive oil or cover with plastic wrap. Then firmly press cooled patty mixture into it. Turn patties out onto baking sheet and bake as usual. These freeze great so I always make a double batch.

Chef Tips

Try some great variations, such as raisins and walnuts, dried blueberries and pecans, or even dried apples, dates, and coconut. Use your imagination, the combinations are endless.

CHERRY-ALMOND OATS

Fruit, Nuts, and Carbs

MAKES 6 SERVINGS
GLUTEN-FREE | SOY-FREE | OIL-FREE

STUFF YOU NEED

3 cups of your favorite vanilla-flavored plant-based milk
See recipes for Vanilla Cashew, Oat, and Rice Milk on pages 196-201

1 cup water

1 cup steel cut oats

1 cup dried cherries

1/2 cup sliced almonds

1/3 cup coconut or turbinado (raw) sugar

1/2 tsp Himalayan pink salt or salt of your choice

LET'S COOK!

1. Bring milk and water to a boil.
2. Add the remainder of ingredients and reduce heat to medium-low.
3. Simmer for approximately 30 minutes, stirring occasionally.
4. Let sit for 5 minutes to cool and thicken.

MINI CRUSTLESS QUICHES

Oui, C'est Magnifique

MAKES 10 TO 12 MINI QUICHES
GLUTEN-FREE | NUT-FREE | OIL-FREE (OPTIONAL)

STUFF YOU NEED

1 small onion, chopped

3 cups broccoli, chopped

1/4 cup water

1 lb firm tofu

1 Tbsp cornstarch

1/4 cup nutritional yeast flakes

1/2 tsp turmeric

1/2 tsp onion powder

1/2 tsp garlic powder

3/4 tsp Himalayan pink salt or salt of your choice

1/2 tsp kala namak (black salt)

1/2 tsp aluminum-free baking powder

2 Tbsps of your favorite plant-based milk
See recipes for Oat and Rice Milk on pages 198-201

LET'S COOK!

1. Preheat oven to 350°F (or 177°C).
2. Add onions and broccoli to a pan and sauté in water until softened.
3. Place the remainder of ingredients in a food processor or high speed blender and process/ blend until smooth.
4. In a bowl, combine tofu mixture and vegetables.
5. Fill oiled muffin tins or a silicone cupcake mold to the top with the mixture.
6. Bake for 25 to 27 minutes.
7. Remove from the oven and let sit for 5 minutes before lifting from tins.
8. Serve warm.

OVEN HASH BROWNS

I ❤ Potatoes

MAKES 4 SERVINGS
GLUTEN-FREE | SOY-FREE | NUT-FREE | OIL-FREE (OPTIONAL)

STUFF YOU NEED

1 1/2 cups onions, chopped

2 1/2 cups potatoes, peeled and grated or processed

2 tsps Himalayan pink salt or salt of your choice (keep 1 tsp separate)

2 Tbsps extra virgin olive oil

LET'S COOK!

1. Preheat oven to 375°F (177°C).
2. Place onions in a bowl.
3. In a separate bowl, toss the grated potatoes with 1 tsp of salt and let sit for 5 minutes. Allow mixture to cool.
4. Squeeze all liquid out of the potatoes with your hands.
5. Add potatoes, remaining salt, and oil to the onions.
6. Toss to coat.
7. Spread evenly on an oiled baking sheet.
8. Bake for 55 to 60 minutes until potatoes are thoroughly cooked.

Chef Tips

If you use coconut milk as a substitute for coconut oil, increase baking time to 35 to 40 minutes.

BANANA-NUT MUFFINS
You'll Go Bananas for These

MAKES 12 MUFFINS
SOY-FREE

STUFF YOU NEED

1 cup coconut sugar or turbinado (raw sugar)

1/2 cup melted coconut oil (or 1/2 cup coconut milk)

2 tsps aquafaba or any egg replacement equivalent to 2 eggs

3 large ripe bananas, mashed

1 tsp vanilla flavoring
See page 10 for the vanilla bean equivalent

1/2 to 1 cup pecans, chopped

1 cup whole wheat pastry flour

1 cup whole wheat flour

1 tsp Himalayan pink salt or salt of your choice

1 Tbsp aluminum-free baking powder

1 tsp lemon juice

LET'S COOK!

1. Preheat oven to 350°F (177°C).
2. Combine all ingredients in a large bowl and mix well.
3. Fill oiled muffin tins or silicone cupcake molds and bake for approximately 22 to 25 minutes.

BLUEBERRY-PECAN QUINOA

Where North and South America Unite

MAKES 4 SERVINGS
TOTAL TIME: 30 MINUTES OR LESS
GLUTEN-FREE | SOY-FREE | OIL-FREE

STUFF YOU NEED

2 cups water

1 cup quinoa, rinsed

Pinch of Himalayan pink salt or salt of your choice

1/4 cup pure maple syrup, honey, or raw blue agave nectar

1/2 cup dried or fresh blueberries

1/2 cup pecans, coarsely chopped

1/4 to 1/2 cup of your favorite plant-based milk (optional)
See recipes for Vanilla Cashew, Oat, and Rice Milk on pages 196-201

LET'S COOK!

1. Bring water to a boil.
2. Add quinoa and salt.
3. Cover and simmer on low for 20 to 22 minutes. Quinoa will be transparent.
4. Add in pure maple syrup, nuts, and blueberries.
5. For a creamier texture, add plant-based milk.

Chef Tips

Refined coconut oil will give these biscuits a more neutral taste instead of virgin coconut oil, which has a dominant coconut flavor. You could also use non-hydrogenated plant butter instead of coconut oil.

COUNTRY BISCUITS AND GRAVY

Southern Comfort Food, But Healthier

MAKES APPROXIMATELY 8 BISCUITS AND 5 CUPS OF GRAVY
SOY-FREE

STUFF YOU NEED

Biscuits

1 cup whole wheat flour

1 cup whole wheat pastry flour

3/4 tsp Himalayan pink salt or salt of your choice

1 Tbsp aluminum-free baking powder

1/4 cup refined coconut oil

3/4 cup of your favorite unsweetened plant-based milk
See recipes for Oat and Rice Milk on pages 198-201.

1 Tbsp lemon juice

Gravy

3/4 cup raw cashews, soaked, drained, and rinsed

4 1/2 cups water

1 1/2 tsps Himalayan pink salt or salt of your choice

3 Tbsps cornstarch

1 Tbsp nutritional yeast flakes

1 tsp onion powder

Grains of Paradise to taste (optional)

LET'S COOK!

Biscuits

1. Preheat oven to 425°F (218°C).
2. Combine dry ingredients in a mixing bowl.
3. Add coconut oil.
4. Use a fork or pastry cutter to crumble.
5. Add in milk and lemon juice and mix until a ball is formed. If sticky, add more flour, a little at a time.
6. Sprinkle flour on counter, take dough out of bowl, and put on counter.
7. Knead dough by pushing it forward, using the palm of your hand, and then folding it backwards.
8. Roll dough out to just under an inch thick.
9. Use a biscuit cutter or a small mason jar lid to cut out biscuits.
10. Place biscuits on an oiled baking sheet, having them touch on the sides for a better rise.
11. Bake on the top rack of the oven for approximately 10 to 12 minutes.

Gravy

12. Blend all ingredients in a high speed blender until smooth.
13. Pour into a saucepan and bring to a boil, whisking constantly until desired thickness is reached.
14. Optional: Once cooked, add a few crumbled "Unsausage" Patties to your gravy for a Southern classic!
See recipe on pages 22-23.

Chef Tips

To turn this recipe into a parfait, layer fresh fruit, then strawberry cream, and lastly granola. Repeat until glass is full.

FANCY FRUIT SALAD WITH STRAWBERRY CREAM

To Be Eaten With That Special Someone

MAKES 6 SERVINGS
TOTAL TIME: 30 MINUTES OR LESS (IF NUTS HAVE BEEN SOAKED IN ADVANCE)
GLUTEN-FREE | SOY-FREE | OIL-FREE

STUFF YOU NEED

1/2 cup raw cashews, soaked, drained, and rinsed

1/2 cup water

2 Tbsps pure maple syrup, honey, or raw blue agave nectar
You can substitute this with 3/4 tsp stevia powder or 6 drops of liquid stevia

2-3 leaves fresh mint (optional)

1/2 cup fresh or frozen strawberries

4 cups fresh fruit cut into bitesize pieces
Banana, apple, pear, kiwi, mango, etc.

1 cup whole berries
Strawberries, blueberries, blackberries, raspberries, etc.

Unsweetened coconut flakes, chopped walnuts, and/or granola for garnish
See recipe for Granola and Dessert Topping on page 18-19

LET'S MIX!

1. Mix nuts, water, sweetener, mint, and strawberries in a blender until smooth.
2. Add fruit to a bowl.
3. Fold in sauce.
4. Refrigerate for about half an hour.
5. Top with coconut, chopped walnuts, or granola to serve.

CORNBREAD MUFFINS

Adding Soul to a Southern Staple

MAKES APPROXIMATELY 10 MUFFINS
SOY-FREE | NUT-FREE

STUFF YOU NEED

1/2 cup whole wheat flour

1/2 cup whole wheat pastry flour

1 cup cornmeal

1 1/2 Tbsps aluminum-free baking powder

1/3 cup extra virgin olive oil

1/4 cup aquafaba

1/3 cup honey

1/2 tsp Himalayan pink salt or salt of your choice

1/2 cup of your favorite plant-based milk
See recipes for Vanilla Cashew, Oat, and Rice Milk on pages 196-201

1/4 cup water

LET'S COOK!

1. Preheat oven to 350°F (177°C).
2. Mix all ingredients in a large bowl. Add oats and cook for about five minutes, stirring constantly.
3. Pour mixture into oiled muffin tins and bake in the oven on the top shelf for 16 to 18 minutes until golden brown.

Entrees

Chef Tips

For a more realistic meaty texture and taste, replace the jackfruit with 3 to 4 king oyster mushroom stems, shredded with a fork. You can purchase king oyster mushrooms at most Asian grocery stores.

PULLED BBQ JACKFRUIT SANDWICH

Calling All BBQ Lovers

MAKES 2-3 SERVINGS
TOTAL TIME: 30 MINUTES OR LESS
GLUTEN-FREE | SOY-FREE | NUT-FREE

STUFF YOU NEED

1 can green jackfruit in brine, drained and very well rinsed (to remove brine flavor)

1 small onion, diced

1/4 cup water

2 Tbsps lemon juice

1 Tbsp cumin

1 tsp thyme

1/2 Tbsp garlic powder

2 Tbsps olive oil (optional)

Himalayan pink salt to taste or salt of your choice

1 cup Sweet and Tangy BBQ Sauce
See recipe on pages 112-113

4 whole grain rolls

Citrus-Cilantro Slaw (optional)
See recipe on pages 86-87

LET'S COOK!

1. Remove all hard pieces from the jackfruit.
2. Using your hands, pull the fruit apart into shreds.
3. Sauté onions in water until they are soft and slightly brown.
4. Add jackfruit and seasonings.
5. Sauté until heated.
6. Add 1 cup of BBQ sauce and optional olive oil.
7. Heat until the sauce is the desired thickness.
8. Serve on your favorite whole wheat roll.
9. Top with Citrus-Cilantro Slaw (optional).

Chef Tips

This plant-based cheese sauce recipe makes a perfectly creamy mac 'n cheese, but that's not the only way you can use it. This sauce is also a great cheese replacement in other dishes, such as nachos, baked potatoes, and broccoli. It even works as the base for a cheesy soup.

MAC 'N CHEESE

Make Your Southern Friends Jealous

MAKES 6 TO 8 SERVINGS
GLUTEN-FREE | SOY-FREE | OIL-FREE

STUFF YOU NEED

1 lb whole grain pasta
I use Tinkyada gluten-free brown rice pasta

Creamy Cheese Sauce
1/3 cup raw cashews, soaked, drained, and rinsed

1 can coconut milk

1/3 cup nutritional yeast flakes

2 tsps Himalayan pink salt or salt of your choice

1/2 tsp onion powder

1/3 cup cornstarch

2 1/2 Tbsps lemon juice

2 cups water

1/2 cup roasted red peppers, canned pimentos, or fresh red pepper

Baked Mac 'n Cheese
1 1/4 cup whole grain breadcrumbs

Fresh parsley for garnish

LET'S COOK!

Mac 'n Cheese

1. Prepare macaroni in a large pot as indicated on the package.
2. Drain and set aside.
3. Place all cheese sauce ingredients in a high speed blender and blend until smooth.
4. Pour mixture into a saucepan and warm up on medium heat, whisking regularly.
5. When desired consistency is reached, mix with cooked macaroni and serve.

Baked Mac 'n Cheese

6. Preheat oven to 350°F (177°C).
7. Mix pasta and cheese sauce together and pour into an oiled baking dish.
8. Top with breadcrumbs or other topping of your choice.
9. Bake for 35 to 40 minutes.
10. Sprinkle with fresh parsley.

Chef Tips

I love pesto. If you need to be somewhat economical when planning meals, this is a delicious and inexpensive version of the traditional basil and pine nut pesto.

SPINACH-WALNUT PESTO PASTA

A Pine Nut-Free Version to Save Some Pennies

MAKES 6 TO 8 SERVINGS
TOTAL TIME: 30 MINUTES OR LESS
GLUTEN-FREE (OPTIONAL) | SOY-FREE

STUFF YOU NEED PASTA

1 lb whole grain pasta
I use Tinkyada gluten-free brown rice pasta

Pesto
4 cups fresh baby spinach leaves

1/2 cup extra virgin olive oil

3 cloves of garlic

1 1/2 tsp lemon juice

1 cup walnuts

1 1/4 tsp Himalayan pink salt or salt of your choice

1/4 cup of your favorite plant-based parmesan cheese or nutritional yeast flakes
See recipe for Parmesan-Like Cheese on pages 176-177

2 finely diced Roma tomatoes

LET'S COOK!

1. In a large pot, prepare pasta as directed on package.
2. Drain and put back in pot.
3. Pulse remaining ingredients except tomatoes in a food processor until completely blended.
4. Mix pesto sauce with pasta.
5. Stir in diced tomatoes and serve.

LASAGNA ROLL-UPS WITH SPINACH RICOTTA

Italian At Its Finest

MAKES 12 TO 15 ROLL-UPS
TOTAL TIME: 30 MINUTES OR LESS (IF NUTS HAVE BEEN SOAKED IN ADVANCE)
OIL-FREE (OPTIONAL)

STUFF YOU NEED

1 box whole grain lasagna sheets

Spinach Ricotta
1 lb firm tofu, rinsed with some water pressed out

2 handfuls (approximately 2 cups) of fresh spinach, finely chopped

1/4 cup walnuts, finely chopped

1/2 cup nutritional yeast flakes

1 Tbsp pure maple syrup, raw blue agave nectar, or honey

1 tsp lemon juice

1 tsp Himalayan pink salt or salt of your choice

1 tsp garlic powder

White Cheese Sauce
1/3 cup raw cashews, soaked, drained, and rinsed

1 can coconut milk

1/3 cup nutritional yeast flakes

2 tsps Himalayan pink salt or salt of your choice

1/2 tsp onion powder

1/3 cup cornstarch

1 Tbsp lemon juice

2 cups water

LET'S COOK!

1. Preheat oven 350°F (177°C).
2. Cook lasagna sheets as directed on package.
3. While lasagna sheets are cooking, place all ingredients for the spinach ricotta except spinach and walnuts into a food processor and combine well.
4. Mix in spinach and walnuts.
5. Place all ingredients for the white cheese sauce in a high speed blender and blend until smooth.
6. Heat up cheese sauce on the stove on medium-high, whisking regularly until desired thickness is reached.
7. In a large baking dish, pour a thin layer of pasta sauce on the bottom and spread evenly to prevent the roll-ups from sticking.
8. To make the roll-ups, spread a thin layer of the spinach ricotta on a lasagna sheet.
9. Add a thin layer of pasta sauce across the ricotta.
10. Roll it up and place on its side in the baking dish.
11. Repeat until you have run out of spinach ricotta. Add a thin layer of pasta sauce across the ricotta.
12. Cover the roll-ups with pasta sauce.
13. Add a thin layer of pasta sauce across the ricotta.
14. Top with 1 cup of white cheese sauce.
15. Bake for 25 minutes.

Chef Tips

A great way to make evenly sized meatless balls is to use a medium-sized cookie scoop. You can find a variety of scoop sizes in the kitchen section of your local discount or department store.

HOMESTYLE SPAGHETTI AND MEATLESS BALLS

That's Italian!

MAKES 6 TO 8 SERVINGS AND 22 TO 24 MEATLESS BALLS
TOTAL TIME: 30 MINUTES OR LESS
OIL-FREE (OPTIONAL)

STUFF YOU NEED

1 lb of your favorite whole grain pasta
I use Tinkyada gluten-free brown rice pasta

Pasta Sauce

1 large onion, finely chopped

8 cloves of garlic, minced

2 cans organic crushed tomatoes

2 tsps Himalayan pink salt or salt of your choice

1 Tbsp honey, raw blue agave nectar, or pure maple syrup

2 Tbsps extra virgin olive oil (optional)

1 bunch of fresh basil, sliced in ribbons

1/4 cup nutritional yeast flakes

Meatless Balls

1 lb firm or extra firm tofu, mashed

3 Tbsps Bragg Liquid Aminos
Use Bragg Coconut Aminos for soy-free option

2 cups whole grain breadcrumbs

2 Tbsps fresh parsley, chopped

1/2 cup pecans, ground

1/2 cup walnuts, ground

1/2 cup onion, finely chopped

1 Tbsp nutritional yeast flakes

1 to 2 cloves of garlic, minced

1 tsp Italian style seasoning

1 tsp onion powder

1/2 tsp garlic powder

3 Tbsps potato or tapioca flour/starch

LET'S COOK!

1. Preheat oven 375°F (191°C).

Spaghetti and Sauce

2. Cook pasta as directed on package.
3. Sauté onion in water until translucent.
4. Add garlic and sauté until softened. Shape into patties and place on an oiled or non-stick cookie sheet.
5. Bake for approximately 12 minutes on each side until lightly browned.
6. Add tomatoes, salt, and sweetener.
7. Bring to a boil.
8. Simmer for 20 minutes.
9. Remove from heat and add olive oil, basil, and nutritional yeast flakes.
10. Add more salt to taste.

Meatless Balls

11. Mix all meatless ball ingredients together in a bowl.
12. The consistency should be such that you can shape it into balls. If it's too soft, add additional breadcrumbs. If it's too dry, add water a Tbsp at a time.
13. Form into balls (I usually make them the size of a golf ball) and bake on an oiled or parchment paper-lined baking sheet for 25 minutes.
14. Flip balls over and cook for an additional 15 minutes. Baking time will depend on the size of the balls.

ANY BEAN VEGGIE BURGER

Where Beans Come Together

MAKES 4 PATTIES
SOY-FREE | NUT-FREE

STUFF YOU NEED

1/4 cup onion, minced

1/4 cup green or red pepper, minced

1/4 cup celery, minced

2/3 cup cooked beans
My favorite is Cannellini beans, also known as white kidney beans

1/3 cup whole grain breadcrumbs

1/4 cup potato starch or instant mashed potato flakes

2 Tbsps water (add more if needed)

1 tsp onion powder

1/2 tsp garlic powder

Himalayan pink salt to taste or salt of your choice

LET'S COOK!

1. Preheat oven to 350°F (177°C).
2. Chop vegetables individually in a food processor.
3. Drain water from the peppers by squeezing them in your hand.
4. Sauté vegetables in water until translucent.
5. Drain beans and mash in a bowl.
6. Mix in breadcrumbs, potato starch, water, and veggies.
7. Shape into patties and place on a plate.
8. Refrigerate for at least a half an hour.
9. Bake on an oiled baking sheet for approximately 12 to 15 minutes on each side.

NOODLES WITH ASIAN-STYLE PEANUT SAUCE

Thai Vibes on a Plate

MAKES 3 TO 4 SERVINGS
TOTAL TIME: 30 MINUTES OR LESS
GLUTEN-FREE | SOY-FREE (OPTIONAL)

STUFF YOU NEED

Noodles
1/2 lb rice noodles
Or any thin noodle of your choice

1 Tbsp sesame oil

Peanut Sauce
1/2 cup peanut butter

1/2 can coconut milk

2 1/2 Tbsps Bragg Liquid Aminos
Use Bragg Coconut Aminos for soy-free option

1 tsp garlic, minced

2 1/2 Tbsps lime juice

1 Tbsp sesame oil

1 Tbsp honey

1 Tbsp ginger, grated

1/2 cup cilantro, chopped

1/2 tsp curry powder
See Mild Curry Powder recipe on pages 182-183

1/3 cup water

Chopped peanuts or cilantro, sliced green onion/scallion or red pepper, or a lime cut in wedges for garnish.

LET'S COOK!

1. Cook noodles as directed on package.
2. Drain and add back to pot.
3. Drizzle about 1 Tbsp of sesame oil to prevent sticking and to add some flavor.
4. Allow mixture to cool.
5. Add all sauce ingredients to a saucepan and whisk over medium heat until warm and well combined.
6. Plate noodles.
7. Top with peanut sauce and garnish.

Chef Tips

To make easy and uniform patties, use a small canning jar lid as a baking ring. To prevent sticking, brush lid with olive oil and then firmly press cooled patty mixture into it. Turn patties out onto cookie sheet and bake as usual.

ZUCCHINI "CRABLESS" CAKES

Your Best Multipurpose Vegetable

MAKES 10 TO 12 CAKES
SOY-FREE | NUT-FREE | OIL-FREE

STUFF YOU NEED

2 medium-sized zucchinis (approximately 2 cups when shredded)

2 cups whole grain breadcrumbs

3 Tbsps potato or tapioca flour/starch or 3 Tbsps aquafaba

3 Tbsps onion, finely chopped

2 Tbsps carrot, grated

1 Tbsp of your favorite plant-based mayo
See recipes for Easy Tofu Mayo, "Aquafabulous" Mayo, and Creamy Cashew Mayo on pages 152-157

2 tsps celery salt

1/2 tsp paprika

1/2 tsp ground bay leaf (optional)

1/2 lemon, juiced or 2 Tbsps lemon juice

1/4 cup flat leaf parsley, chopped

LET'S COOK!

1. Preheat oven to 375°F (191°C).
2. Grate zucchinis and place in a colander over a bowl.
3. Sprinkle lightly with salt.
4. Allow zucchinis to drain for about 30 minutes.
5. Press zucchinis down to remove excess water.
6. Pat dry with paper towels. It should be moist but not wet.
7. In a medium-sized bowl, mix zucchinis, onions, carrots, and breadcrumbs.
8. In a small bowl, mix flour/starch or aquafaba, plant-based mayo, seasonings, lemon juice, and parsley.
9. Mix with zucchini mixture.
10. Add a little water if too dry.
11. Form mixture into balls with your hands.
12. Press down to form patties.
13. Place on an oiled or parchment paper-lined baking sheet.
14. Bake for 15 minutes on each side.

Chef Tips

Cornflakes are not made with wheat, but they do sometimes contain barley malt, which contains gluten. Look for cornflakes without malt if you are sensitive to gluten.

NOT REALLY MEATLOAF

You'll Loaf This So Much

MAKES 6 SERVINGS
GLUTEN-FREE (OPTIONAL)

STUFF YOU NEED

1/4 cup potato flour/starch or instant mashed potato flakes mixed with 3/4 cup warm water

1 cup walnuts, finely chopped

1 lb firm tofu, mashed

1 Tbsp Bragg Liquid Aminos
Use Bragg Coconut Aminos for soy-free option

2 Tbsps extra virgin olive oil

1 1/2 cups corn flakes, crushed

1 small onion, chopped

1 tsp Wright's Liquid Smoke

LET'S COOK!

1. Preheat oven to 350°F (177°C).
2. In a sauté pan, sauté onions in water until softened.
3. In a large bowl, mix the sautéd onions together with the remainder of the ingredients and spoon into an oiled loaf pan.
4. Press down. Then, using a spatula, push loaf away from sides of pan.
5. Bake for 1 hour.

STUFFED ZUCCHINI

Warning: Bursting With Flavor

MAKES 6 SERVINGS
GLUTEN-FREE | SOY-FREE (OPTIONAL) | OIL-FREE (OPTIONAL)

STUFF YOU NEED

6 small/medium zucchinis

3/4 cup of your favorite tomato sauce
See tomato sauce from Homestyle Spaghetti and Meatless Balls recipe on pages 50-51

1/3 cup onions, chopped

2 Tbsps nutritional yeast flakes

1 tsp dried basil

1 tsp dried oregano

1 tsp Himalayan pink salt or salt of your choice

1 cup brown rice, cooked

1/4 cup Butler Soy Curls, broken into bite-size pieces (optional)

3/4 cup white cheese sauce from Lasagna Roll-Ups With Spinach Ricotta recipe
See pages 48-49

LET'S COOK!

1. Preheat oven to 350°F (177°C).
2. Cut each zucchini in half and scoop out the middle.
3. Place scooped out zucchinis in a pot with tomato sauce, onions, seasonings, rice, and optional Soy Curls.
4. Heat on medium-high for 15 minutes until Soy Curls are softened and mixture thickens. Stir frequently.
5. Place zucchini boats on an oiled or parchment paper lined baking sheet and stuff with filling.
6. Top with white cheese sauce and bake for 20 to 25 minutes until zucchini is tender.

Chef Tips

To kick this up a notch, you can add one cup of bite-sized Butler Soy Curls that you have rehydrated in your favorite chicken-like seasoning (or see recipe for Chicken-Like Seasoning on pages 178-179).

VEGETABLE JAMBALAYA

A Veggie Medley

MAKES 6 SERVINGS
GLUTEN-FREE | SOY-FREE | NUT-FREE | OIL-FREE (OPTIONAL)

STUFF YOU NEED

1 medium red or green pepper, chopped

1 medium onion, chopped

1 celery stick, chopped

5 cloves of garlic, minced

Water to sauté

2 cups water

1 can (14.5 ounces) diced tomatoes (undrained)

1 can (8 ounces) tomato sauce

1 tsp Italian seasoning

1 to 1 1/2 tsps Himalayan pink salt or salt of your choice

1 tsp fennel seed, crushed

1 cup brown rice, dextrinized

1 can (16 ounces) lima or butter beans, rinsed and drained

1 can (16 ounces) red kidney beans, rinsed and drained

1 Tbsp extra virgin olive oil (optional)

LET'S COOK!

1. In a large pot, add pepper, onion, and celery, and sauté in 2 to 4 Tbsps of water until tender. If the vegetables begin to dry out, add a little more water.
2. Add garlic and cook for another minute.
3. Add two cups of water, tomatoes, tomato sauce, and seasonings to the pot.
4. Bring to a boil, then stir in rice.
5. Reduce heat, cover, and let simmer for about 20 minutes or until liquid is absorbed and the rice is tender.
6. Stir in beans and heat through.
7. Drizzle with olive oil.

COCONUT-TOFU CURRY WITH CAULIFLOWER "RICE"

For a Low-Carb Day

MAKES 4 SERVINGS
GLUTEN-FREE | NUT-FREE

STUFF YOU NEED

Tofu
1 lb firm or extra firm tofu

1 tsp extra virgin olive oil

1 Tbsp Bragg Liquid Aminos
Use Bragg Coconut Aminos for soy-free option

1/2 tsp garlic powder

3 Tbsps cornstarch

Coconut Curry Sauce
2 Tbsps fresh ginger, grated

3 Tbsps garlic, minced

1 Tbsp Mild Curry Powder
See recipe on pages 182-183

1/2 tsp Himalayan pink salt or salt of your choice

1 onion, thinly sliced

1 cup carrots, peeled and sliced in circles

1 cup broccoli florets, chopped

1 can (16 ounces) diced tomatoes

1 can (13.5 ounces) coconut milk

1/2 cup vegetable broth or 1/2 cup water with 1 Tbsp your favorite chicken-like seasoning
See recipe for Chicken-Like Seasoning on pages 178-179

Cauliflower "Rice"
1 cauliflower head, grated or finely processed

1/4 cup water

1/4 tsp Himalayan pink salt or salt of your choice

LET'S COOK!

1. Preheat oven to 400°F (204°C).

Tofu

2. Cut tofu into cubes and place in a gallon-sized plastic bag with olive oil, Bragg Liquid Aminos, and garlic powder.
3. Mix together.
4. Add cornstarch and shake well to coat tofu.
5. Bake in the oven for 30 minutes, turning tofu after 15 minutes so that it browns evenly.

Coconut Curry Sauce

6. While tofu is baking, sauté ginger and garlic in water until fragrant.
7. Add curry powder and salt.
8. Stir in onions and cook until softened for about 5 to 6 minutes.
9. Continue to add water as needed so that the onion doesn't stick.
10. Stir in carrots, diced tomatoes, coconut milk, and broth.
11. Simmer covered for about 12 to 15 minutes until carrots can be easily pierced with a fork.
12. Uncover for about 3 to 5 minutes to thicken.
13. Add in tofu and serve over cauliflower "rice".

Cauliflower "Rice"

14. Heat sauté pan on medium/high heat.
15. Add 1/4 cup of water.
16. Add cauliflower.
17. Mix and cook for approximately 3 minutes, stirring frequently.
18. Once cooked, stir in salt.
19. Ladle curry sauce onto cauliflower rice.
20. Top with tofu cubes.

Chef Tips

For the best texture, I use 1 1/4 cups old fashioned rolled oats and 1 cup quick oats.

To make uniform patties, use a large canning jar lid as a mold. To prevent sticking, brush lid with olive oil and then firmly press cooled patty mixture into it. Turn patties out onto a baking sheet and bake as usual. Freeze leftovers for another quick meal.

OAT BURGERS

Like Fast Food, But Healthy

MAKES APPROXIMATELY 8 PATTIES

GLUTEN-FREE | SOY-FREE (OPTIONAL) | OIL-FREE (OPTIONAL)

STUFF YOU NEED

1/4 cup walnuts, ground

1/4 cup raw sunflower seeds, ground

2 1/4 cups water

2 Tbsps Bragg Liquid Aminos
Use Bragg Coconut Aminos for soy-free option

2 tsps of your favorite chicken-like seasoning
See recipe for Chicken-Like Seasoning on pages 178-179

1 tsp Italian seasoning

1 Tbsp nutritional yeast flakes

1/2 medium onion, finely chopped

2 1/4 cups oats (use gluten-free oats if needed)

LET'S COOK!

1. Preheat to oven 350°F (177°C).
2. Add all ingredients, except oats, to a large pot and bring to a boil.
3. Stir in oats until moistened.
4. Let mixture cool enough to handle.
5. Form patties and place on an oiled or parchment paper-lined baking sheet.
6. Bake for 40 minutes, 20 minutes on each side, or until slightly browned.
7. This makes a good batch of burgers, so you can freeze any leftover patties. Just defrost overnight and reheat.

Chef Tips

For those of you who love garlic, you can always swap out the garlic powder for a fresh clove or two. To slice vegetables julienne style, simply cut into small matchstick-like slices.

CREAMY PASTA PRIMAVERA

A Colorful Splash of Spring

MAKES APPROXIMATELY 8 PATTIES
GLUTEN-FREE (OPTIONAL) | OIL-FREE

STUFF YOU NEED

Pasta
1 lb whole grain pasta
I use Tinkyada gluten-free brown rice pasta

1 red pepper, cut into strips

1 onion, halved, then sliced

1 cup broccoli, cut into small florets

1 yellow squash, sliced in half moons

1 to 2 carrots, julienned

1/4 cup water or more if needed

1 cup Butler Soy Curls, broken into bite-size pieces (optional)

1 to 2 Tbsps of your favorite chicken-like seasoning
See recipe for Chicken-Like Seasoning on pages 178-179

Creamy Sauce
1 cup raw cashews, soaked, drained, and rinsed

1/2 tsp Himalayan pink salt or salt of your choice

1 Tbsp garlic powder

1 Tbsp of your favorite chicken-like seasoning
See recipe for Chicken-Like Seasoning on page 178-179

1 1/2 Tbsps nutritional yeast flakes

2 Tbsps whole wheat flour
Or corn starch for gluten-free option

1/3 cup of your favorite plant-based parmesan cheese
See recipe for Parmesan-Like Cheese on pages 176-177

3 1/2 cups water

LET'S COOK!

1. Sauté vegetables on high in a large sauté pan with water, adding additional water as needed until vegetables are softened.
2. If you use Soy Curls, rehydrate them in water with 1 to 2 Tbsps chicken-like seasoning on high heat until softened.
3. Drain any excess water and add Soy Curls to softened vegetables.
4. Add all sauce ingredients to a high speed blender and blend on high for 30 to 45 seconds until everything is combined and the sauce is smooth.
5. Pour creamy sauce into a saucepan and heat on medium-high, whisking constantly until thickened.
6. Add in cooked vegetables and Soy Curls.
7. Add to your favorite whole grain rotini pasta.

Soups, Stews, and Salads

CREAMY BEAN FLORENTINE SOUP

Cool Beans

MAKES 8 SERVINGS
TOTAL TIME: 30 MINUTES OR LESS
GLUTEN-FREE | SOY-FREE | NUT-FREE | OIL-FREE

STUFF YOU NEED

6 cups cooked white beans or 5 cans white beans
Navy beans, great northern beans, etc.

8 cups vegetable broth

1 large onion, chopped

2 carrots, chopped

1 tsp garlic, minced

1 tsp dried basil

1 Tbsp Himalayan pink salt or salt of your choice

1 bag fresh spinach, chopped

LET'S COOK!

1. Add onions, carrots, and garlic to a large pot and sauté with a little bit of broth until vegetables are softened.
2. Drain beans in a colander.
3. Add beans and remaining ingredients (except spinach) to the large pot.
4. Cover and cook on medium heat for 15 to 20 minutes.
5. Once finished, remove 2 to 3 cups of beans and broth.
6. Blend in a high speed blender until creamy.
7. Pour back into pot and mix.
8. Add chopped spinach and serve.

Chef Tips

Eliminate the potato and add whole grain noodles for a classic chicken noodle soup.

HEARTY "CHICKENLESS" VEGETABLE SOUP

Make It a Souper Day

MAKES 6 TO 8 SERVINGS
TOTAL TIME: 30 MINUTES OR LESS
GLUTEN-FREE | SOY-FREE (OPTIONAL) | NUT-FREE | OIL-FREE

STUFF YOU NEED

4 celery stalks, chopped

1 onion, chopped

6 cups water (divide into 3 bowls, 2 containing 1/2 cup and 1 containing 5 cups)

1/4 cup of your favorite chicken-like seasoning
See recipe for Chicken-Like Seasoning on pages 178-179

4 potatoes, peeled and cubed

3 carrots, peeled and sliced

1 cup Butler Soy Curls, broken into bite-size pieces
Substitute with 1 cup cooked garbanzo beans, drained, for soy-free option.

2 cups garbanzo beans with liquid

1 Tbsp nutritional yeast flakes

1 tsp Himalayan pink salt or salt of your choice

3 Tbsps fresh parsley, chopped

LET'S COOK!

1. In a large pot, simmer celery and onions in a 1/2 cup of water mixed with chicken-like seasoning until vegetables are tender.
2. Add 5 cups of water, potatoes, carrots, and Butler Soy Curls (or 1 cup of garbanzo beans, drained, for soy-free option) to the pot.
3. In a high speed blender, mix together the remaining 2 cups of garbanzo beans with liquid, nutritional yeast, salt, and 1/2 cup of water until smooth.
4. Stir garbanzo bean mixture into the pot.
5. Simmer for 20 minutes on medium heat.
6. If needed, add additional water to get desired consistency.
7. Top with parsley and serve.

LEMONY "CHICKENLESS" RICE SOUP

Zest Recipe Ever

MAKES 6 SERVINGS
GLUTEN-FREE | NUT-FREE | OIL-FREE

STUFF YOU NEED

1 medium onion, chopped

3 carrots, thinly sliced

2 cloves of garlic, minced

8 cups water

3 Tbps of your favorite chicken-like seasoning
See recipe for Chicken-Like Seasoning on pages 178-179

2 tsps lemon zest, loosely packed

1 tsp lemon juice

3/4 cup brown rice, dextrinized

1 cup Butler Soy Curls, broken into bite-size pieces

1 tsp Himalayan pink salt or salt of your choice

1/2 cup flat leaf parsley, chopped

LET'S COOK!

1. In a large soup pot, sauté onions, carrots, and garlic in a little bit of water until tender.
2. Add additional water, if needed, so that the vegetables don't stick to the pot.
3. Add the remaining water, chicken-like seasoning, lemon zest, and lemon juice, and salt. Then bring to a boil.
4. When the water boils, add rice and Soy Curls.
5. Reduce to medium heat and simmer covered until rice is tender. Add water if needed for a thinner soup.
6. Top with parsley and serve.

Chef Tips

Wow! This recipe has the longest list of ingredients in this book, but I promise you that it is easy to make, and definitely worth it!

MINESTRONE SOUP
Invented By Vegetable-Loving Italians

MAKES 8 SERVINGS
GLUTEN-FREE | SOY-FREE | NUT-FREE | OIL-FREE (OPTIONAL)

STUFF YOU NEED

1 medium onion, minced

2 zucchinis, sliced in quarters

1/2 lb green beans, trimmed and cut into 1/2 inch pieces

2 celery stalks, cut into small pieces

5 cloves of garlic, minced

4 cups vegetable broth

3 medium potatoes, diced

1 1/2 cups red kidney beans, cooked

1 1/2 cups small white beans, cooked

8 plum or Roma tomatoes, diced small

4 carrots, peeled and cut into bite-size pieces

2 Tbsps dried parsley

1 1/2 tsps dried oregano

1 Tbsp Himalayan pink salt or salt of your choice

1 bay leaf

1 tsp dried basil

1/2 tsp dried thyme

1/2 tsp rosemary

2 Tbsps nutritional yeast flakes

6 cups hot water

8 oz fresh baby spinach, chopped

1 1/2 cups small or medium whole grain pasta shells
I use Tinkyada gluten-free brown rice pasta

2 Tbsps hot water

LET'S COOK!

1. Place onion, celery, garlic, green beans, and zucchini in a pot on medium heat and sauté in water for about 5 minutes, or until the onions become translucent.
2. Add the vegetable broth, potatoes, tomatoes, beans, carrots, hot water, and seasonings to the pot.
3. Bring to a boil. Then reduce heat and simmer for 20 minutes.
4. Add spinach leaves and pasta.
5. Cook for an additional 20 minutes.
6. Remove bay leaf from soup.
7. Mix in olive oil before serving.

Chef Tips

As a child, this was a summer favorite for my family and I. Growing up we always had an abundance of zucchinis and tomatoes that we grew in our garden. This recipe brings back wonderful memories.

RUSTIC ZUCCHINI STEW

This Is How We Stew It

MAKES 4 SERVINGS
TOTAL TIME: 30 MINUTES OR LESS
GLUTEN-FREE | SOY-FREE | NUT-FREE

STUFF YOU NEED

1/4 cup water

2 medium onions, sliced into half circles

6 Roma tomatoes, cubed

6 medium zucchinis, cut into half moons

1 to 1 1/2 Tbsps dried oregano

2 Tbsps extra virgin olive oil

2 tsps Himalayan pink salt or salt of your choice

Your favorite plant-based parmesan cheese for garnish (optional)
See recipe for Parmesan-Like Cheese on pages 176-177

LET'S COOK!

1. In a large pot, sauté onions in water until softened.
2. Add tomatoes, zucchinis, and salt.
3. Heat on high until vegetables become tender.
4. Add oregano and olive oil.
5. Top with plant-based parmesan cheese to garnish (optional).

INDIAN LENTIL STEW

A Protein-Packed Flavor Explosion

MAKES 4 SERVINGS
GLUTEN-FREE | SOY-FREE | NUT-FREE | OIL-FREE

STUFF YOU NEED

2 cups dry lentils

1 large onion, chopped

6 carrots, peeled and cut into chunks

4 celery sticks, cut into chunks

4 potatoes, cubed

4 cups vegetable broth

1 tsp Himalayan pink salt or salt of your choice

1/4 tsp garlic powder

1 tsp onion powder

1 Tbsp Mild Curry Powder recipe
See recipe on pages 182-183

Water (as needed)

LET'S COOK!

1. Rinse lentils thoroughly.
2. Place into a pot together with the onion.
3. Cover with broth.
4. Bring to a boil and cook for about 10 minutes.
5. Add carrots, celery, potatoes, and seasonings.
6. If it cooks down, add more water if necessary.
7. Cook on medium heat for approximately 20 minutes.
8. If it's too thick, add more water. If it's too thin, cook uncovered for an additional 10 minutes until stew thickens.

CAPRESE SALAD WITH DRESSING

Mamma Mia, Deliziosa!

MAKES 4 SERVINGS
TOTAL TIME: 30 MINUTES OR LESS (IF THE "MOCK-ZZARELLA" HAS BEEN MADE IN ADVANCE)
GLUTEN-FREE | SOY-FREE

STUFF YOU NEED

Salad
4 Roma tomatoes, cut into small cubes or sliced

16 basil leaves, cut into ribbons

"Mock-zzarella" Cheese cut into approximately 30 small cubes or slices
See recipe on pages 188-189

Dressing
2 Tbsps extra virgin olive oil

1 tsp lemon juice

1/2 tsp Himalayan pink salt or salt of your choice

LET'S MIX!

1. In a bowl, combine together cubed tomatoes, cheese, and basil or arrange slices on a plate alternating tomatoes and cheese.
2. Top with basil.
3. In a small, separate bowl, whisk together olive oil, lemon juice, and salt.
4. Pour dressing over salad and toss or drizzle dressing over slices.

CITRUS-CILANTRO SLAW

Just Cut and Mix

MAKES 4 SERVINGS
TOTAL TIME: 30 MINUTES OR LESS
GLUTEN-FREE | SOY-FREE | NUT-FREE

STUFF YOU NEED

2 1/2 cups green and/or purple cabbage, shredded or chopped

1/2 cup carrots, grated

1/2 cup cilantro, chopped

2 to 3 limes, juiced, or 6 Tbsps lime juice

3 Tbsps honey or raw blue agave nectar

2 tsps extra virgin olive oil

Himalayan pink salt to taste or salt of your choice

LET'S COOK!

1. Combine cabbage, carrot, and cilantro in a bowl.
2. In a separate bowl, mix together lime juice, sweetener, olive oil, and salt.
3. Add dressing to vegetables and mix. Allow mixture to cool.
4. Refrigerate for 1 hour.

SOUTHWESTERN "CHICKENLESS" SALAD

A Cowboy's Favorite

MAKES 4 SERVINGS
TOTAL TIME: 30 MINUTES OR LESS
GLUTEN-FREE | NUT-FREE (OPTIONAL) | OIL-FREE (OPTIONAL)

STUFF YOU NEED

1 1/2 cups Butler Soy Curls, broken into bite-size pieces

2 Tbsps of your favorite chicken-like seasoning
See recipe for Chicken-Like Seasoning on pages 178-179

3 cups water

3/4 cup diced celery

1/2 cup diced onion

1/4 cup diced red pepper

1/4 cup fresh cilantro, chopped

1 cup of your favorite plant-based mayo
See recipes for Easy Tofu, "Aquafabulous" Mayo, and Creamy Cashew on pages 152-157

2 to 3 Tbsps Taco Seasoning
See recipe on pages 180-181

2 Tbsps lime juice

LET'S COOK!

1. In a medium saucepan, bring water and chicken-like seasoning to a boil.
2. Rehydrate Butler Soy Curls.
3. Drain and squeeze out excess water.
4. Chop Soy Curls to desired size.
5. Add to a bowl and mix in celery, onion, red pepper, and cilantro.
6. In a separate bowl, whisk together Taco Seasoning, mayo, and lime juice.
7. Combine all and mix.
8. Refrigerate until ready to serve.

Chef Tips

This dish is perfect on crackers or a sandwich. It is super realistic in texture and flavor. I have also made stuffed eggs with this recipe before, using egg shaped molds for the eggless whites.

AMAZING EGGLESS SALAD
An "Eggcellent" Choice

MAKES 4 TO 8 SERVINGS
TOTAL TIME: 30 MINUTES OR LESS
GLUTEN-FREE | NUT-FREE (OPTIONAL) | OIL-FREE (OPTIONAL)

STUFF YOU NEED

Eggless Whites
2 cups of your favorite unsweetened plant-based milk (almond or soy work best)

2 tsps agar-agar powder

1/2 tsp kala namak (black salt)

Eggless Yolks
1 cup (8 oz) firm or extra firm tofu (not silken)

1/4 cup your favorite plant-based mayo
See recipes for Easy Tofu, "Aquafabulous" Mayo, and Creamy Cashew on pages 152-157

1 tsp lemon juice

1/4 tsp Himalayan pink salt or salt of your choice

3/4 tsp turmeric

1/2 tsp kala namak (black salt)

2 celery stalks, finely chopped

1/4 cup red onion, chopped (optional)

Additional plant-based mayo if needed

LET'S COOK

1. Combine milk, agar-agar powder, and kala namak in a saucepan and bring to a boil.
2. Pour into a 9x13 inch baking pan.
3. Refrigerate for 20 to 30 minutes until hardened.
4. Once hardened, use a knife to cut the eggless whites into small cubes or use a fork to mash into small pieces.
5. Add to a mixing bowl.
6. Add eggless yolk ingredients to a high speed blender and process until creamy.
7. Add to eggless whites.
8. Combine, then mix in celery and optional onion and if needed additional mayo for a creamy and spreadable consistency.

"TOFU-NA" MACARONI SALAD

Something's Fishy About This

MAKES 8 SERVINGS
TOTAL TIME: 30 MINUTES OR LESS IF TOFU HAS BEEN PREPARED A DAY IN ADVANCE
GLUTEN-FREE (OPTIONAL) | OIL-FREE (OPTIONAL)

STUFF YOU NEED

1 lb whole grain elbow macaroni
I use Tinkyada gluten-free brown rice pasta

1 lb firm or extra firm tofu (frozen overnight, then defrosted)

1/2 cup onion, finely chopped

1/2 cup celery stalks, finely chopped

1/4 cup carrots, grated

1 cup of your favorite plant-based mayo
See recipes for Easy Tofu, "Aquafabulous" Mayo, and Creamy Cashew on pages 152-157

2 Tbsps Bragg Liquid Aminos
Use Bragg Coconut Aminos for soy-free option

1 Tbsp lemon juice

2 Tbsps kelp powder

LET'S COOK!

1. Remove tofu from container.
2. Drain and press out all water, then place in a quart-sized ziplock bag.
3. Place in freezer and freeze overnight.
4. Remove from freezer and let completely defrost.
5. Press out all water from thawed tofu, discard water, and crumble into a bowl.
6. Cook macaroni according to package.
7. Drain and set aside in a large bowl.
8. Add Bragg Liquid Aminos and lemon juice to tofu. Mix well.
9. Add the macaroni and the remainder of the ingredients to the bowl and mix.

CRANBERRY-NUT GARBANZO SALAD

Ingredients Meant to Bean Together

MAKES 6 SERVINGS
TOTAL TIME: 30 MINUTES OR LESS
GLUTEN-FREE | SOY-FREE | OIL-FREE

STUFF YOU NEED

Dressing

1/4 cup of your favorite plant-based mayo or tahini
See recipes for Easy Tofu, "Aquafabulous" Mayo, and Creamy Cashew on pages 152-157

3 Tbsps apple juice

1 to 2 Tbsps lemon juice

2 Tbsps water

2 Tbsps honey, raw blue agave nectar, or pure maple syrup

Salad

2 1/2 cups cooked garbanzo beans, drained and rinsed

3/4 cup celery, finely chopped

1/3 cup dried cranberries, chopped

1/3 cup pecans, chopped

1/3 cup green onions/scallions, sliced

1/4 to 1/2 tsp Himalayan pink salt or salt of your choice

LET'S COOK!

Dressing

1. Combine mayo or tahini, apple juice, lemon juice, water, and sweetener in a small bowl.
2. Whisk together and refrigerate until needed.

Salad

3. Add garbanzo beans to a large bowl.
4. Roughly mash with a fork or potato masher.
5. Add celery, cranberries, nuts, scallions, and salt.
6. Mix together.
7. Add dressing and mix well.

Sides and Sauces

CAULIFLOWER-RANCH MASHERS

A Creamy Cruciferous Combo

MAKES 4 SERVINGS
TOTAL TIME: 30 MINUTES OR LESS
GLUTEN-FREE | OIL-FREE (OPTIONAL)

STUFF YOU NEED

1 head of cauliflower, cut into florets

1 cup of your favorite plant-based mayo
See recipes for Easy Tofu, "Aquafabulous" Mayo, and Creamy Cashew on pages 152-157

2 tsps lemon juice

2 Tbsps ranch seasoning from Ranch Seasoning and Dressing recipe
See pages 184-185

LET'S COOK!

1. Steam cauliflower.
2. In a small bowl, mix together mayo, lemon juice, and ranch seasoning, creating a ranch mayo.
3. In a large bowl, mash cauliflower with a potato masher or fork until desired consistency is reached.
4. Combine ranch mayo with cauliflower and mix together. You can also combine all ingredients in a food processor or high speed blender and pulse until smooth with some bits and chunks left over. Do not completely puree.

Chef Tips

This is my American version of my absolute favorite dish that I had while doing mission work in Samoa. The original native dish is called palusami and is normally made with taro leaves. Spinach, being much easier to find in western countries, makes a great substitute.

SOUTH PACIFIC SPINACH

A Westernized Island Bake

MAKES 4 SERVINGS
GLUTEN-FREE | SOY-FREE | NUT-FREE | OIL-FREE

STUFF YOU NEED

1 10 oz bag of fresh spinach

1 can coconut cream
Substitute with the coconut cream from 2 cans of full fat coconut milk, removing only the cream from the cans

1 medium-sized onion, chopped

Himalayan pink salt to taste or salt of your choice

LET'S COOK!

1. Preheat oven to 350°F (177°C).
2. In a 9x13 inch baking dish, layer spinach and then onions. Repeat until pan is full. It's ok if it's very full because the spinach will shrink.
3. Sprinkle with salt.
4. Add coconut cream.
5. Bake covered for 40 to 45 minutes.

SPANISH RICE
A European Flavor Explosion

MAKES 6-8 SERVINGS
GLUTEN-FREE | SOY-FREE | NUT-FREE | OIL-FREE

STUFF YOU NEED

1/4 medium-sized onion, chopped

1/4 green or red pepper, chopped

3 cloves of garlic, finely chopped

2 cups brown rice, dextrinized

3 cups vegetable broth or water with your favorite chicken-like seasoning
See recipe for Chicken-Like Seasoning on pages 178-179

1 8 oz can tomato sauce

1/2 tsp dried oregano

1/4 cup green olives, chopped or sliced (optional)

LET'S COOK!

1. In a large pot, cook the pepper and onion in a little water until tender. If the vegetables begin to dry out, add a little more water.
2. Add garlic and cook for 1 more minute.
3. Add rice and the remainder of the ingredients to the pot with vegetables.
4. Stir and bring to a boil.
5. Once it starts to boil, turn the heat to low and cover.
6. Let it simmer for 20 to 25 minutes until rice is tender.
7. Fluff with a fork and serve.

HARVEST QUINOA PILAF
A Fall Dish to Warm You Up

MAKES 6-8 SERVINGS
GLUTEN-FREE | SOY-FREE | OIL-FREE

STUFF YOU NEED

2 cups sweet potatoes, peeled and cubed

2 cups butternut squash, peeled and cubed

6 cloves of garlic, minced

2 cups quinoa, cooked

1/2 cup pecans, chopped

1/3 cup dried cranberries

1/2 tsp Himalayan pink salt or salt of your choice

1 tsp maple flavoring or 2 Tbsps pure maple syrup

1/4 cup sunflower seeds, ground

3 Tbsps fresh sage, chopped

2 Tbsps coconut oil, melted

Fresh sage, chopped, for garnish

LET'S COOK!

1. Preheat oven to 425 °F (218 °C).
2. Mix sweet potatoes, squash, and garlic in a bowl with 1 Tbsp of coconut oil.
3. Roast in a baking pan for 25 minutes, stirring occasionally.
4. Sprinkle with chopped pecans and roast for five more minutes.
5. In a separate bowl, mix cooked quinoa with remaining coconut oil, 3 Tbsps of sage, maple flavoring or syrup, and salt.
6. Stir in sweet potatoes and butternut squash.
7. Garnish with additional sage.

SWEET AND DELICIOUS ORANGE-CRANBERRY SAUCE

A Spin on a Holiday Staple

MAKES 1 1/2 CUPS
TOTAL TIME: 30 MINUTES OR LESS
GLUTEN-FREE | SOY-FREE | NUT-FREE | OIL-FREE

STUFF YOU NEED

12 oz package of fresh cranberries

1/2 cup raw blue agave nectar or honey or 1/3 cup stevia powder

3/4 cup water

Zest of 2 oranges

1/2 tsp vanilla flavoring
Or see page 10 for the vanilla bean equivalent

LET'S COOK!

1. Combine all ingredients in a medium saucepan.
2. Bring to a boil, then reduce heat.
3. Simmer for 10 minutes until cranberries burst and mixture thickens.
4. Cool and enjoy.

Chef Tips

I use Yukon Gold or Red Bliss potatoes because they have a thin skin. Keeping the skin on adds lots of fiber and nutrients to the dish. Feel free to use any type of potato, but don't forget to preferably keep the skin on.

GARLIC-MASHED POTATO MIX-UP

A Tater Twister

MAKES 10 SERVINGS
TOTAL TIME: 30 MINUTES OR LESS (IF NUTS HAVE BEEN SOAKED IN ADVANCE)
GLUTEN-FREE | SOY-FREE | OIL-FREE

STUFF YOU NEED

3 lbs Yukon Gold or Red Bliss potatoes, cubed (leaving the skin on is optional)

1 head of cauliflower, cut into florets

1/4 cup raw cashews or your favorite unsweetened plant-based milk
See recipes for Oat and Rice Milk on pages 198-201

4 to 5 cloves of garlic, peeled

1 tsp Himalayan pink salt or salt of your choice

1 tsp of your favorite chicken-like seasoning
See recipe for Chicken-Like Seasoning on pages 178-179

2 Tbsps nutritional yeast flakes

Extra unsweetened plant-based milk if mix-up is too thick

LET'S COOK!

1. Add cubed potatoes to a pot and cover with water.
2. Boil until potatoes are softened.
3. Drain water and set aside.
4. Add cauliflower, ~~potatoes~~, cashews, and garlic to a pot of water and bring to a boil. If you use milk instead of cashews, don't add the milk at this step.
5. Cook for about 8 minutes until softened.
6. Once softened, drain the cauliflower mix and add to a blender with salt, chicken-like seasoning, and nutritional yeast. If you did not use cashews, add the milk at this step.
7. Blend until smooth and creamy.
8. Mash potatoes until desired consistency is reached.
9. Add cauliflower mix from the blender to the potatoes and mix gently. If it's too thick, add some unsweetened plant-based milk until desired consistency is reached.

RATATOUILLE
A Vegetable Rainbow

MAKES 8 SERVINGS
TOTAL TIME: 30 MINUTES OR LESS
GLUTEN-FREE | SOY-FREE | NUT-FREE

STUFF YOU NEED

1 8 oz can of tomato sauce

1/2 small onion, chopped

1 small eggplant, thinly sliced

2 zucchinis, thinly sliced

2 yellow squash, thinly sliced

2 small red peppers, deseeded and sliced in thin circles

1/2 tsp Himalayan pink salt or salt of your choice

4 cloves of garlic, minced

2 tsps dried basil

3/4 tsp dried thyme

3/4 tsp dried rosemary

1/2 tsp dried oregano

3 Tbsps extra virgin olive oil

LET'S COOK!

1. Preheat oven to 375°F (191°C).
2. Use a deep dish pie plate or square baking pan, and cover the bottom with tomato sauce and chopped onion.
3. Begin layering the vegetables next to each other, alternating varieties and overlapping.
4. If you use a pie plate, start from the outside and make a spiral of vegetables.
5. If you use a square baking pan, make rows instead.
6. You should be able to see the colorful edges of each vegetable.
7. Sprinkle evenly with garlic, dried herbs, and salt.
8. Drizzle with olive oil.
9. Cover with parchment paper (cut to the size of the dish), and then aluminum foil.
10. Bake for approximately 45 minutes until vegetables are tender.

SWEET AND TANGY BBQ SAUCE

The Boss of the Sauce

MAKES 1 1/4 CUP
TOTAL TIME: 30 MINUTES OR LESS
GLUTEN-FREE | SOY-FREE (OPTIONAL) | NUT-FREE

STUFF YOU NEED

1/2 cup apple or pineapple juice

1/4 cup pure maple syrup

1 can tomato paste (or a small 8 oz can of tomato sauce)

2 Tbsps blackstrap molasses

2 Tbsps Bragg Liquid Aminos
Use Bragg Coconut Aminos for soy-free option

3 Tbsps lemon juice

1 1/4 tsp ginger, minced

1 clove of garlic, minced

1 tsp smoked paprika

1/2 tsp cumin

1 tsp Wright's Hickory Liquid Smoke

2 Tbsps extra virgin olive oil

LET'S COOK!

1. Add all ingredients to a high speed blender and blend until smooth.
2. Pour mixture into a saucepan and heat on medium-high heat until thickened. Stir frequently.

Chef Tips

This is a great sauce to use as a topping or even a salad dressing if thinned out with a little water. It goes great as a sandwich spread or on top of falafels and even as a delicious vegetable dip.

TZATZIKI SAUCE
Cool as a Cucumber

MAKES 1 1/4 CUP
TOTAL TIME: 30 MINUTES OR LESS
GLUTEN-FREE | SOY-FREE | NUT-FREE (OPTIONAL) | OIL-FREE

STUFF YOU NEED

2 cups of your favorite plant-based sour cream
See Simple Sour Cream recipe on pages 168-169

1 cup cucumber, seeded and diced

2 Tbsps lemon juice

2 cloves of garlic, minced

2 Tbsps fresh dill, finely chopped

Himalayan pink salt or salt of your choice to taste

LET'S MIX!

1. Mix all ingredients together and refrigerate.

Chef Tips

For a brown gravy variation, use the above recipe, but omit the salt and nutritional yeast and add 1 Tbsp Bragg Liquid Aminos. (Choose Bragg Coconut Aminos for soy-free option.)

TRADITIONAL GRAVY

A Holiday Staple

MAKES 2 1/2 CUPS
TOTAL TIME: 30 MINUTES OR LESS (IF NUTS HAVE BEEN SOAKED IN ADVANCE)
GLUTEN-FREE | SOY-FREE (OPTIONAL) | OIL-FREE

STUFF YOU NEED

2 cups water

1/2 cup raw cashews, soaked, drained, and rinsed

1 Tbsp cornstarch

1 tsp onion powder

1/2 tsp garlic powder

1 tsp Himalayan pink salt or salt of your choice

1 Tbsp nutritional yeast flakes

2 tsps of your favorite chicken-like seasoning
See recipe for Chicken-Like Seasoning on pages 178-179.

LET'S COOK!

1. Blend all ingredients together in a high speed blender until very smooth.
2. Pour into a saucepan and bring to a boil, whisking constantly until thickened.

MAPLE APPLE SAUCE

A Taste of the North

MAKES 2 1/2 CUPS
TOTAL TIME: 30 MINUTES OR LESS
GLUTEN-FREE | SOY-FREE | NUT-FREE | OIL-FREE

STUFF YOU NEED

8 apples, peeled and cut into pieces

1/4 cup water

2 Tbsps pure maple syrup

1/2 tsp coriander (optional)

1/4 tsp cardamom (optional)

LET'S COOK!

1. Add apple pieces and water to a large saucepan.
2. Bring to a boil, then reduce heat to maintain a simmer.
3. Cover and cook, stirring once or twice, until the apples are very soft (about 30 minutes).
4. With a potato masher or fork, mash the apples to the desired consistency and stir in pure maple syrup and optional seasonings.

ROASTED TOMATO SALSA

Chip Chip Hooray!

MAKES 2 1/2 TO 3 CUPS
TOTAL TIME: 30 MINUTES OR LESS
GLUTEN-FREE | SOY-FREE | NUT-FREE

STUFF YOU NEED

6 plum or Roma tomatoes

1 onion, quartered

2 to 3 cloves of garlic

1 Tbsp extra virgin olive oil

3 to 4 Tbsps fresh cilantro

2 to 3 Tbsps fresh lime juice

LET'S COOK!

1. Preheat oven to 400°F (204°C).
2. Place tomatoes, garlic, and onions on a non-stick baking sheet.
3. Drizzle with olive oil and toss.
4. Roast in the oven for 20 to 25 minutes.
5. Add roasted vegetables to a food processor together with salt, cilantro, and lime juice, and pulse until desired consistency is reached.
6. Refrigerate for about 20 minutes so that flavors can meld together and salsa can cool.
7. Serve with your favorite baked tortilla chips.

CORN AND BLACK BEAN SALSA

Don't Get "Cornfused", Here's the Recipe

MAKES 3 CUPS
TOTAL TIME: 30 MINUTES OR LESS
GLUTEN-FREE | SOY-FREE | NUT-FREE | OIL-FREE

STUFF YOU NEED

1 1/4 cup fresh or frozen corn or 1 can whole kernel corn, drained

1 1/2 cups black beans or 1 can black beans, drained and rinsed

4 plum tomatoes, seeded and chopped

1/2 medium red onion, chopped

1 bunch fresh cilantro, minced

1 to 2 limes, juiced, or 2 to 4 Tbsps lime juice

Himalayan pink salt to taste or salt of your choice

1 avocado, cubed for garnish

LET'S COOK!

1. In a large bowl, combine all ingredients except avocado.
2. Cover and refrigerate until ready to serve.
3. Top with avocado.
4. Serve with baked tortilla chips.

Desserts

Chef Tips

To make easy and uniform patties, use a small canning jar lid as a baking ring. To prevent sticking, brush lid with olive oil and then firmly press cooled patty mixture into it. Turn patties out onto cookie sheet and bake as usual.

BANANA-DATE-NUT COOKIES

You'll Go Nuts Over 'Em

MAKES 24 COOKIES
GLUTEN-FREE (OPTIONAL) | SOY-FREE | OIL-FREE (OPTIONAL)

STUFF YOU NEED

4 ripe bananas

2 3/4 cups quick oats
Use gluten-free oats if needed

1 1/3 cup dates, chopped

3/4 cup walnuts, chopped
Or any nut of your choice

3/4 cup shredded, unsweetened coconut

3/4 cup raisins or dried cranberries

2 Tbsps honey, raw blue agave nectar, or pure maple syrup

1 1/2 tsp vanilla flavoring
Or see page 10 for the vanilla bean equivalent

1 tsp Himalayan pink salt or salt of your choice

1/4 cup extra virgin olive oil (optional)

LET'S COOK!

1. Preheat oven 350°F (177°C).
2. In bowl, mash bananas and add remaining ingredients. Mix well.
3. Refrigerate for approximately 15 minutes.
4. Drop a spoonful onto an oiled or parchment paper-lined baking sheet.
5. Flatten the mixture with a fork.
6. Bake on the middle rack of the oven for approximately 25 to 30 minutes or until browned.
7. Remove from baking sheet and let cool on rack.

Chef Tips

You can make this a nut-free candy by replacing the nut butter with sunflower seed butter and eliminating chopped peanuts.

CARIN'S CHOCOLATY CHUNKY CAROB CANDY CLUSTERS

To Satisfy Your Sweet Tooth

MAKES 16 TO 20 SERVINGS
TOTAL TIME: 30 MINUTES OR LESS
GLUTEN-FREE | SOY-FREE | NUT-FREE (OPTIONAL) | OIL-FREE

STUFF YOU NEED

2 cups carob chips
Regularly sweetened, barley malt sweetened, or unsweetened

1 cup all natural creamy peanut butter
Optional: almond, cashew, or sunflower seed butter

1 cup raisins

1 cup chopped peanuts (optional if you want to make it nut-free)

1/2 cup shredded, unsweetened coconut, divided

LET'S COOK!

1. Melt carob chips and peanut butter in a heavy-bottom saucepan.
2. Once melted, remove from heat and stir in raisins, peanuts, and 1/4 cup shredded coconut.
3. Spread in a 9x9 inch parchment paper-lined baking dish or mini cupcake tins with liners.
4. Top with remaining shredded coconut.
5. Refrigerate or freeze for 20 minutes.
6. Remove from parchment paper and cut into squares or serve in cupcake liners.
7. Store in ziplock bag in freezer.

CAROB-HAZELNUT MOUSSE

Chocoholics Unite!

MAKES 2 SERVINGS
GLUTEN-FREE | SOY-FREE | OIL-FREE

STUFF YOU NEED

3/4 cup hazelnuts

1 can coconut milk

2 Tbsps carob powder

1 tsp caffeine-free grain coffee (optional)
Such as Roma, Pero, etc.

1/2 cup dates, pitted and softened in warm water

1 tsp vanilla flavoring
See page 10 for vanilla bean equivalent

Pinch of Himalayan pink salt or salt of your choice

2 Tbsps roasted hazelnuts, chopped for garnish

1 Tbsp carob chips, chopped for garnish

LET'S COOK!

1. Preheat oven to 350°F (177 Celcius).
2. Roast hazelnuts on a baking sheet until slightly browned. Stir occasionally.
3. Add roasted hazelnuts, coconut milk, carob powder, coffee substitute (optional), dates, vanilla flavoring, and salt to a high speed blender and blend until smooth (about 1 minute).
4. Pour into serving dishes and refrigerate.
5. Garnish with chopped hazelnuts and carob chips.

PECAN-CAROB CHIP COOKIES

That's One Smart Cookie!

MAKES 2 1/2 TO 3 DOZEN COOKIES
SOY-FREE

STUFF YOU NEED

1 cup whole wheat flour

1 cup whole wheat pastry flour

2 1/2 tsps aluminum-free baking powder

1/2 tsp Himalayan pink salt or salt of your choice

1 cup coconut or turbinado (raw) sugar

1 Tbsp blackstrap molasses

1/2 cup coconut oil, melted

6 Tbsps water

1/3 cup creamy cashew or almond butter

1 Tbsp vanilla flavoring
See page 10 for the vanilla bean equivalent

1 cup carob chips
Sweetened, barley malt sweetened, or unsweetened

1/2 cup chopped pecans

LET'S COOK!

1. Preheat oven to 350°F (177°C).
2. In a large bowl, mix together both types of flour, baking powder, and salt.
3. In a separate bowl, mix together sugar, coconut oil, water, nut butter, and vanilla flavoring.
4. Combine flour with wet ingredients.
5. Mix in carob and nuts.
6. Let cookie dough sit at room temperature for approximately 1 hour.
7. Use a small cookie scoop to portion dough about 1 inch apart on an oiled or parchment paper-lined baking sheet.
8. Bake for 12 to 15 minutes until golden brown.

SUMMER FRUIT CRUMBLE

It's Berry Nice, You'll "A-peach-iate" It

MAKES 10 TO 12 SERVINGS
GLUTEN-FREE | SOY-FREE

STUFF YOU NEED

1 1/4 cup apple juice

2 Tbsps cornstarch

1 tsp lemon juice

1/4 cup raw blue agave nectar or honey

4 cups fresh or frozen peaches, defrosted

2 cups fresh or frozen blueberries, defrosted

2 to 4 cups unbaked granola from Granola and Dessert Topping recipe
See pages 18-19

1 to 2 Tbsps coconut oil to coat baking dish

LET'S COOK!

1. Preheat oven to 350°F (117°C).
2. Coat a 9x13 inch baking dish with coconut oil and place the peaches in it.
3. Top with blueberries and set aside.
4. Combine apple juice and cornstarch in a small saucepan.
5. Whisk together until completely dissolved.
6. Cook over medium heat until thickened.
7. Add lemon juice and sweetener, then mix well.
8. Remove mixture from heat and pour over blueberries and peaches. Toss well.
9. Top with unbaked granola.
10. Bake for 30 to 40 minutes or until granola is golden brown and fruit is bubbling.
11. Let cool, then serve.

Chef Tips

To make great lemon bars, increase the cornstarch to 1/3 cup and pour the prepared mixture over your favorite pre-baked crust. Refrigerate to harden.

LEMON PUDDING

Pucker Up

MAKES 6 SERVINGS
GLUTEN-FREE | SOY-FREE | NUT-FREE | OIL-FREE

STUFF YOU NEED

3 Tbsps cornstarch

1/3 cup orange juice

1 cup pineapple juice

1 can coconut milk

1/4 cup honey or raw blue agave nectar

1/3 cup lemon juice

1 tsp lemon zest

1/2 tsp lemon flavoring

1/4 tsp Himalayan pink salt or salt of your choice

2 Tbsps shredded unsweetened coconut for topping (optional)

Coconut Whipped Cream for topping (optional)
See recipe on pages 190-191

LET'S COOK!

1. Place all ingredients in a saucepan, whisk to dissolve cornstarch, and then bring to a boil.
2. Remove from heat and pour into a dessert cup.
3. Refrigerate for 4 to 5 hours to properly thicken.
4. Sprinkle shredded unsweetened coconut on pudding or top with Coconut Whipped Cream (optional).

TROPICAL CHIA DELIGHT
A Superfood Dessert

MAKES 6 SERVINGS
GLUTEN-FREE | SOY-FREE | NUT-FREE (OPTIONAL) | OIL-FREE

STUFF YOU NEED

1/4 cup chia seeds

1 can coconut milk

1 can crushed pineapple or 2 1/2 cups fresh pineapple, processed

1/4 cup honey or raw blue agave nectar (optional)

1/4 cup shredded unsweetened coconut, toasted

1/4 cup macadamia nuts, roasted and chopped (optional)

LET'S COOK!

1. In a sauté pan on medium heat, toast coconut until light brown. Set aside.
2. In a mixing bowl, combine chia seeds, coconut milk, pineapple, and sweetener.
3. Pour into a serving bowl or individual serving dishes.
4. Refrigerate for 2 hours.
5. When ready to serve, top with toasted coconut and optional macadamia nuts.

Chef Tips

To make this a gluten-free recipe, use 3 cups of unbaked granola from the Granola and Dessert Topping recipe in place of the topping in this recipe (see pages 18-19).

PEAR AND APPLE CRISP

What a Great Pear

MAKES 8 TO 10 SERVINGS
SOY-FREE | OIL-FREE

STUFF YOU NEED

Filling
1 cup apple juice

3 apples, peeled and sliced or cubed

3 pears, peeled and sliced or cubed

1/4 cup honey, raw blue agave nectar, or turbinado (raw) sugar

1/2 cup raisins (optional)

1/2 tsp coriander

1/4 tsp cardamom

2 Tbsps cornstarch

1/4 cup water

Topping
1/2 tsp Himalayan pink salt or salt of your choice

1 tsp vanilla flavoring
See page 10 for the vanilla bean equivalent.

2 3/4 cups quick rolled oats
Use gluten-free oats if needed.

1/4 cup extra virgin olive oil

1/2 cup raisins (optional)

1/2 tsp coriander

1/4 cup whole wheat flour

1/2 cup walnuts, chopped, or shredded unsweetened coconut (optional)

LET'S COOK!

1. Preheat oven to 350°F (117°C).
2. Add filling ingredients except cornstarch and water to a saucepan.
3. Cook on medium-high heat until fruit is soft.
4. Mix 2 Tbsps of cornstarch with cold water to make a slurry.
5. Add slurry to the fruit mixture and thicken mixture.
6. Pour into a 9x13 inch baking dish.
7. Mix topping ingredients in a bowl and sprinkle over fruit.
8. Bake for approximately 45 minutes or until golden brown.

CHRISTMAS CAROB-PEPPERMINT BARK

No Trees Were Hurt in the Process

MAKES 16 SERVINGS
TOTAL TIME: 30 MINUTES OR LESS
GLUTEN-FREE | SOY-FREE | OIL-FREE

STUFF YOU NEED

2 cups carob chips
Regularly sweetened, barley malt sweetened, or unsweetened

1 cup all natural creamy almond or cashew butter

3/4 cup sliced almonds

3/4 cup dried cranberries or cherries, chopped

1 to 1 1/2 tsps peppermint flavoring

1/4 cup shredded unsweetened coconut for topping

LET'S COOK!

1. Melt carob chips and nut butter in a heavy-bottom saucepan.
2. Once melted, remove from heat and stir in fruit, almonds, and peppermint flavoring.
3. Spread onto a parchment paper-lined jelly roll pan, baking sheet, or casserole dish.
4. Top with coconut flakes.
5. Refrigerate or freeze for 20 minutes.
6. Break into pieces.
7. Store in a ziplock bag in the freezer.

Chef Tips

To make a delicious peanut butter cookie, just use peanut butter instead of almond butter and top with chopped peanuts instead of almonds.

ALMOND BUTTER COOKIES
A Nutty Treat

MAKES 18 COOKIES
TOTAL TIME: 30 MINUTES OR LESS
GLUTEN-FREE | SOY-FREE | OIL-FREE

STUFF YOU NEED

1 cup almond flour

1/4 cup pure maple syrup, honey, or raw blue agave nectar

2/3 cup almond butter

2 tsps aluminum-free baking powder

1 tsp almond flavoring

1 to 2 Tbsps almond milk or your favorite plant-based milk
See recipes for Vanilla Cashew, Oat, and Rice Milk on pages 196-201

18 almonds

LET'S COOK!

1. Preheat oven to 325°F (163°C).
2. Combine flour, sweetener, almond butter, baking powder, and almond flavor in a bowl and mix.
3. Add almond or plant-based milk a Tbsp at a time to make a consistency like that of dough.
4. Roll batter into balls, then flatten on a baking sheet that has not been greased.
5. Place 1 almond in the center of each cookie.
6. Bake on the top rack of the oven for approximately 12 minutes.
7. Remove from oven and let cool on the baking sheet.

OLD-FASHIONED APPLE CAKE

A Festive Fall Dessert

MAKES 12 SERVINGS
SOY-FREE | OIL-FREE

STUFF YOU NEED

2/3 cup aquafaba

1 1/4 cup coconut sugar, turbinado (raw) sugar, or any dry sweetener of your choice

1 tsp ground coriander

1/2 tsp cardamom

1/2 cup of your favorite apple sauce
Or see Maple Apple Sauce recipe on pages 118-119

6 medium apples cored, peeled, and cubed

1/2 cup walnuts, chopped

1 tsp vanilla flavoring
Or see page 10 for the vanilla bean equivalent

1 1/4 cups whole wheat flour

3/4 cup whole wheat pastry flour

1 Tbsp aluminum-free baking powder

1/2 tsp Himalayan pink salt or salt of your choice

LET'S COOK!

1. Preheat oven to 350°F (177°C).
2. In large bowl, mix together aquafaba, sweetener, seasonings, apple sauce, apples, walnuts, and vanilla flavoring.
3. In a second bowl, combine remainder of the dry ingredients.
4. Slowly add the dry ingredients to the wet ingredients.
5. Combine thoroughly, then pour batter into an oiled 9x13 inch baking dish and bake for 55 minutes.

RICE PUDDING
A Simple Family Favorite

MAKES 10 TO 12 SERVINGS
GLUTEN-FREE | SOY-FREE | NUT-FREE | OIL-FREE

STUFF YOU NEED

5 cups brown rice, cooked

3 cups of your favorite plant-based milk
See recipes for Vanilla Cashew, Oat, and Rice Milk on pages 196-201

1/2 cup raisins (optional)

1 Tbsp vanilla flavoring
See page 10 for the vanilla bean equivalent

1/2 tsp Himalayan pink salt or salt of your choice

1/2 cup pure maple syrup

Ground cardamon for garnish (optional)

LET'S COOK!

1. Preheat oven to 350°F (117°C).
2. Mix all ingredients in a large bowl.
3. Pour into a 9x13 inch baking dish.
4. Cover with parchment paper, top with foil, and bake for 30 minutes.
5. Take off covers and bake for 20 more minutes until pudding browns on top.
6. Serve warm or refrigerate to thicken.
7. Top with a very light sprinkle of ground cardamom (optional).

Dips and Dressings

TASTY TOFU MAYO

Easy Three-Step Mayonnaise

MAKES 1 1/2 CUPS
TOTAL TIME: 30 MINUTES OR LESS
GLUTEN-FREE | NUT-FREE | OIL-FREE

STUFF YOU NEED

1 12.3 oz box silkened firm tofu (or 1 1/2 cups)

2 tsps onion powder

1 1/2 Tbsps lemon juice

2 tsps nutritional yeast flakes

1/2 to 1 tsp Himalayan pink salt or salt of your choice

1/2 tsp honey or raw blue agave nectar (optional)

LET'S BLEND!

1. Add all ingredients to a high speed blender.
2. Blend until smooth and creamy.
3. Refrigerate to thicken before serving.

"AQUAFABULOUS" MAYO

Where Have You Bean All My Life?

MAKES 1 CUP
TOTAL TIME: 30 MINUTES OR LESS
GLUTEN-FREE | SOY-FREE | NUT-FREE

STUFF YOU NEED

1 Tbsp lemon juice

1 tsp Himalayan pink salt or salt of your choice

3 Tbsps aquafaba

3/4 to 1 cup neutral flavored oil
Grape seed, sunflower, etc.

LET'S BLEND

1. In a high speed blender, blend lemon juice, salt, and aquafaba.
2. While still blending, slowly pour in oil. You will notice that it starts to thicken.
3. Remove from blender and store in a glass jar with lid in the refrigerator before serving. Mayo will thicken up more in refrigerator.

Chef Tips

For this recipe, it is important to soak the cashews first to obtain a creamy texture. Cashew mayo is not as smooth as tofu mayo, so this step is essential.

CREAMY CASHEW MAYO

Spread the Word: It's Delicious

MAKES 1 1/2 TO 2 CUPS
TOTAL TIME: 30 MINUTES OR LESS (IF NUTS HAVE BEEN SOAKED IN ADVANCE)
GLUTEN-FREE | SOY-FREE | OIL-FREE

STUFF YOU NEED

1 1/2 cups raw cashews, soaked, drained, and rinsed

1 Tbsp lemon juice

1 tsp nutritional yeast flakes

3/4 to 1 tsp Himalayan pink salt or salt of your choice

1/2 cup + 2 Tbsps water

LET'S BLEND!

1. Add all ingredients to a high speed blender.
2. Blend until smooth and creamy.
3. Refrigerate to thicken before serving.

"KRAZY" DELICIOUS KETCHUP

Let's Ketchup

MAKES 1 CUP
TOTAL TIME: 30 MINUTES OR LESS
GLUTEN-FREE | NUT-FREE

STUFF YOU NEED

8 oz can tomato sauce

3 Tbsps tomato paste

1 to 2 Tbsps honey, raw blue agave nectar, or pure maple syrup

1 Tbsp lemon juice

1 tsp Bragg Liquid Aminos
Use Bragg coconut aminos for soy-free option

1 Tbps extra virgin olive oil

1 tsp onion powder

1/8 tsp garlic powder

LET'S MIX!

1. Whisk all ingredients together.
2. Refrigerate before serving.

Chef Tips

This is a basic recipe for hummus. You can mix in any other ingredients you'd like for endless varieties, such as roasted red peppers, sun-dried tomatoes, olives, etc. If you buy raw sesame seeds, make sure to toast them in a skillet with no oil or water. Stir frequently until brown to avoid burning.

GARLIC HUMMUS

Experience the Mediterranean at Home

MAKES 3 CUPS
TOTAL TIME: 30 MINUTES OR LESS
GLUTEN-FREE | SOY-FREE | NUT-FREE

STUFF YOU NEED

3 cups or 2 14 oz cans chickpeas, drained

3 to 4 cloves of garlic

1/4 cup lemon juice

1/4 cup tahini or 1/3 cup sesame seeds, toasted

1/3 cup extra virgin olive oil

2 tsps Himalayan pink salt or salt of your choice

1/2 cup water

Paprika for garnish

Additional water if hummus is too thick

LET'S COOK!

1. Add all ingredients except paprika to a blender or food processor.
2. Blend until smooth and the desired consistency has been reached.
3. Add additional water if it's too thick.
4. Garnish with paprika.
5. Serve with warm pita triangles.

Chef Tips

Frozen spinach is cheaper than fresh spinach. The leaves are wilted and flash frozen so when it's defrosted or cooked it does not shrink. It's the best bang for your buck in the frozen foods section at your local grocery store.

CREAMY SPINACH-ARTICHOKE DIP AND STUFFED BREAD

Let's Get to the Heart of the Matter

MAKES 2 CUPS
TOTAL TIME: 30 MINUTES OR LESS
GLUTEN-FREE | SOY-FREE (OPTIONAL) | NUT-FREE (OPTIONAL) | OIL-FREE (OPTIONAL)

STUFF YOU NEED

Dip

1/2 cup of your favorite plant-based mayo
See recipes for Easy Tofu, "Aquafabulous", and Creamy Cashew Mayo on pages 152-157

1/2 cup of your favorite plant-based parmesan cheese
See recipe for Parmesan-Like Cheese on pages 176-177

1/2 cup canned or marinated artichoke hearts, drained and chopped

12 oz package frozen chopped spinach, defrosted, and drained well

2 tsps lemon juice

To Make Stuffed Bread

Your favorite whole wheat bread dough recipe

LET'S COOK!

Dip

1. In a medium-sized bowl, mix all ingredients together.
2. Refrigerate before serving.
3. You can also heat this dish up for a warm dip.

Turn it Into Stuffed Bread

4. Prepare your favorite whole wheat bread dough.
5. Knead the dough, then split into two pieces.
6. Roll out and place onto an oiled baking sheet.
7. Spread filling onto dough.
8. Bake until browned on top.

Chef Tips

Use as a creamy plant-based cheese sauce or a great dip served either hot or cold with baked tortilla chips.

POTATO CHEESE DIP

Just Cook and Blend

MAKES 3 TO 4 CUPS
TOTAL TIME: 30 MINUTES OR LESS
GLUTEN-FREE | SOY-FREE | NUT-FREE

STUFF YOU NEED

2 to 3 potatoes, peeled and cubed

2 to 3 carrots, peeled and sliced

1/2 onion, cut in chunks

Water to cover vegetables, about 1 inch

1/2 cup water

1/3 cup extra virgin olive oil

1 1/2 tsps Himalayan pink salt or salt of your choice

1 Tbsp lemon juice

1/2 cup nutritional yeast flakes

1/4 tsp garlic powder

1/4 tsp onion powder

1/2 tsp of your favorite chicken-like seasoning
See recipe for Chicken-like seasoning on pages 178-179

LET'S COOK!

1. Boil potatoes, carrots, and onions in water until softened.
2. Drain water.
3. Add vegetables to a high speed blender together with the remaining ingredients.
4. Blend until smooth.

Chef Tips

To make a great veggie dip or sandwich spread, reduce water by 1/2 cup.

GARLIC-HERB DRESSING

Warning: Avoid Kissing After Consumption

MAKES 2 CUPS
TOTAL TIME: 30 MINUTES OR LESS (IF SEEDS HAVE BEEN SOAKED IN ADVANCE)
GLUTEN-FREE | SOY-FREE | NUT-FREE | OIL-FREE

STUFF YOU NEED

1 cup raw sunflower seeds, soaked, drained, and rinsed

1 cup water

1/2 tsp Himalayan pink salt or salt of your choice

1 Tbsp raw blue agave nectar, pure maple syrup, or honey

3 Tbsps lemon juice

2 to 3 cloves of garlic

1/4 cup fresh basil

1/4 cup fresh parsley

1 tsp onion powder

Additional water to create a thinner dressing (optional)

LET'S BLEND!

1. Blend all ingredients until smooth and creamy.
2. Add additional water for a thinner dressing, if desired.
3. Refrigerate before serving.

Chef Tips

For a nut-free version, replace cashews with an additional 1/3 cup of raw sunflower seeds.

SIMPLE SOUR CREAM

The Power of Sour

MAKES 2 CUPS
TOTAL TIME: 30 MINUTES OR LESS (IF NUTS HAVE BEEN SOAKED IN ADVANCE)
GLUTEN-FREE | SOY-FREE | OIL-FREE

STUFF YOU NEED

3/4 cup water

1/3 cup raw cashews, soaked, drained, and rinsed

1/3 cup raw sunflower seeds, soaked, drained, and rinsed

3 Tbsps lemon juice

1/2 tsp Himalayan pink salt or salt of your choice

1/2 tsp onion powder

1/4 tsp garlic powder

LET'S COOK!

1. Blend all ingredients in a high speed blender until smooth.
2. Refrigerate to chill and thicken.

Chef Tips

I like to call this liquid guacamole. It even goes great on nachos or anything else that could use a little guac.

AVOCADO-LIME DRESSING

AKA Liquid Guacamole

MAKES 1 1/2 CUPS
TOTAL TIME: 30 MINUTES OR LESS
GLUTEN-FREE | SOY-FREE | NUT-FREE | OIL-FREE

STUFF YOU NEED

2 avocados, peeled and pitted

4 Tbsps lime juice

1 tsp Himalayan pink salt or salt of your choice

1/2 cup onion

1/2 cup chopped cilantro

1/4 to 1/2 cup water

LET'S BLEND!

1. Blend all ingredients in a high speed blender until smooth.
2. Adjust water amount to get desired consistency.
3. Refrigerate.

Chef Tips

If you buy raw sesame seeds, make sure to toast them in a skillet with no oil or water. Stir frequently until browned to avoid burning.

SESAME-GINGER DRESSING

A Taste of Asia

MAKES 1 1/4 TO 1 1/2 CUPS
TOTAL TIME: 30 MINUTES OR LESS
GLUTEN-FREE | SOY-FREE (OPTIONAL)

STUFF YOU NEED

1 Tbsp fresh ginger, chopped

1/2 cup pineapple juice

1 celery stalk, coarsely chopped

2 small carrots, coarsely chopped

1/2 cup peanut butter

2 Tbsps Bragg Liquid Aminos
Use Bragg Coconut Caminos for soy-free option

2 Tbsps lemon juice

3 cloves of garlic

1 1/2 tsps Himalayan pink salt or salt of your choice

2 Tbsps honey

1/2 small onion

2 Tbsps sesame oil or 1/2 cup sesame seeds, toasted

LET'S COOK!

1. Blend all ingredients in a high speed blender until smooth.
2. Add water, if necessary, to achieve desired consistency.
3. Refrigerate before serving.

Seasonings, Smoothies, and Other Stuff

Chef Tips

You can use raw sesame seeds for this recipe, however when it's toasted it adds great depth of flavor to the cheese. If you buy raw sesame seeds, make sure to toast them in a skillet with no oil or water. Stir frequently until browned to avoid burning.

PARMESAN-LIKE CHEESE

It's Grate!

MAKES 1/2 CUP
TOTAL TIME: 30 MINUTES OR LESS
GLUTEN-FREE | SOY-FREE | OIL-FREE

STUFF YOU NEED

1/4 cup cashews, roasted

1/4 cup sesame seeds, toasted

1 1/2 Tbsps nutritional yeast flakes

1/4 to 1/2 tsp Himalayan pink salt or salt of your choice
Only if you use unsalted cashews

1/2 tsp garlic powder

1 tsp lemon juice

LET'S BLEND!

1. Add all ingredients to a high speed blender and blend for 20 to 30 seconds to make a powdery mix.
2. Store in the refrigerator in an airtight container.

Chef Tips

Use in any recipe where chicken-like seasoning is needed. To make a broth, add 1/2 to 1 Tbsps of seasoning to 1 cup hot water.

CHICKEN-LIKE SEASONING

Savory and "Flavory"

MAKES 3/4 CUP
TOTAL TIME: 30 MINUTES OR LESS
GLUTEN-FREE | SOY-FREE | NUT-FREE | OIL-FREE

STUFF YOU NEED

3/4 cup nutritional yeast flakes

1 1/2 Tbsps onion powder

1 tsp garlic powder

1/2 tsp turmeric

1/2 tsp celery seed

1 tsp oregano

1 tsp basil

2 tsps Himalayan pink salt or salt of your choice

1 tsp coconut sugar or turbinado (raw) sugar

1 Tbsp dried parsley

LET'S BLEND!

1. Add all ingredients except parsley to a blender and process until a powdery consistency is formed.
2. Add dried parsley and mix.

TACO SEASONING

Absolutely "Spec-taco-lar!"

MAKES 1/4 CUP
TOTAL TIME: 30 MINUTES OR LESS
GLUTEN-FREE | SOY-FREE | NUT-FREE | OIL-FREE

STUFF YOU NEED

2 Tbsps paprika or smoked paprika

2 Tbsps cumin

1 Tbsp coriander

1 Tbsp Himalayan pink salt or salt of your choice

1 Tbsp garlic powder

1 Tbsp onion powder

2 tsps oregano

LET'S MIX!

1. Whisk ingredients together.
2. Store in an airtight container.

MILD CURRY POWDER

Gentle Flavors of the East

MAKES 1/4 CUP
TOTAL TIME: 30 MINUTES OR LESS
GLUTEN-FREE | SOY-FREE | NUT-FREE | OIL-FREE

STUFF YOU NEED

2 Tbsps ground coriander

1 Tbsp cumin

2 tsps turmeric

1 tsp ground ginger

1 tsp garlic powder

1/2 tsp cardamom

LET'S MIX!

1. Whisk ingredients together.
2. Store in an airtight container.

Chef Tips

Mix Simple Sour Cream (see recipe on pages 168-169), some lemon juice, and some Ranch Seasoning together for a great ranch salad dressing. Add water to achieve desired consistency as needed. Works great as a veggie dip, too.

RANCH SEASONING

Bonus: Ranch Dressing

MAKES 3/4 CUP
TOTAL TIME: 30 MINUTES OR LESS
GLUTEN-FREE | SOY-FREE | NUT-FREE | OIL-FREE

STUFF YOU NEED

2 Tbsps onion powder

2 tsps celery salt

1 Tbsp dried parsley flakes

2 Tbsps dried dill weed

1 tsp garlic powder

1 tsp dried basil

1 tsp Himalayan pink salt or salt of your choice

1/8 tsp stevia powder or 1 tsp coconut sugar

LET'S MIX!

1. Whisk ingredients together.
2. Store in an airtight container

STRAWBERRY-CHIA JAM

No Refined Sugars Here

MAKES 3 CUPS
GLUTEN-FREE | SOY-FREE | NUT-FREE | OIL-FREE

STUFF YOU NEED

2 cups apple juice

2 Tbsps cornstarch

16 oz strawberries, chopped
(approximately 3 cups)

2 Tbsps honey, raw blue agave nectar, or pure maple syrup

1 tsp lemon juice

2 Tbsps chia seeds

LET'S COOK!

1. In a saucepan, mix cornstarch and juice until dissolved.
2. Add remaining ingredients except chia seeds and bring to boil, stirring frequently.
3. Add mixture to a high speed blender and blend until desired smoothness is reached.
4. Add chia seeds to mixture.
5. Pour into a glass container or jelly jar and cool to room temperature.
6. Refrigerate to thicken.

Chef Tips

This recipe requires agar-agar powder. If you use agar-agar flakes instead, you should use 1 1/2 Tbsps for this recipe. Also, to make a great shredded cheese to top pizza, etc., just freeze the block of cheese before shredding.

"MOCK-ZZARELLA" CHEESE

Ciao Fromaggio

MAKES 8 SERVINGS
GLUTEN-FREE | SOY-FREE

STUFF YOU NEED

1 1/2 tsps agar-agar powder

1 cup water, divided

1/3 cup raw cashews, soaked, drained, and rinsed

3 Tbsps tapioca flour/starch

1 tsp lemon juice

1 1/2 tsps nutritional yeast

1/4 tsp garlic powder

1/4 tsp Himalayan pink salt or salt of your choice

LET'S COOK

1. In a saucepan, bring 1/2 cup water to a boil together with agar-agar powder.
2. Cook for 1 minute until mixture has a syrup-like consistency.
3. Add agar-agar mixture and remaining ingredients to a blender. Blend for 1 minute until mixture is smooth.
4. Pour into a saucepan and warm up on medium heat until mixture becomes thick and stretchy.
5. Pour into an oiled container or cheese mold and refrigerate for approximately 1 hour until firm.

COCONUT WHIPPED CREAM

Make Every Dessert Special

MAKES 2 1/2 TO 3 CUPS
TOTAL TIME: 30 MINUTES OR LESS (IF COCONUT CREAM/ MILK HAS BEEN REFRIGERATED OVERNIGHT)
GLUTEN-FREE | SOY-FREE | NUT-FREE | OIL-FREE

STUFF YOU NEED

1 can coconut cream
Substitute with the coconut cream from 2 cans of full fat coconut milk, removing only the cream from the cans

1 tsp vanilla flavoring
See page 10 for the vanilla bean equivalent

1/2 to 1 tsp stevia powder or 3 to 4 Tbsps of your favorite dry sweetener

LET'S MIX!

1. Chill canned coconut cream or milk in the refrigerator overnight.
2. Open the can and scrape out solids into a chilled bowl.
3. Whip with mixer, adding sweetener and vanilla flavoring.
4. Use immediately or refrigerate.

HAPPY APPLE PIE SMOOTHIE

An American Classic in a Glass

MAKES: 2 SERVINGS
TOTAL TIME: 30 MINUTES OR LESS (IF NUTS HAVE BEEN SOAKED IN ADVANCE)
GLUTEN-FREE | SOY-FREE | OIL-FREE

STUFF YOU NEED

1/2 cup apple juice

1/2 cup of your favorite plant-based milk
See recipes for Vanilla Cashew, Oat, and Rice Milk on pages 196-201

1/2 cup raw cashews, soaked, drained, and rinsed

2 apples, peeled and cubed

1/4 tsp cardamom

1/2 tsp coriander

1 Tbsp vanilla flavoring
See page 10 for the vanilla bean equivalent

2 to 3 Tbsps pure maple syrup, honey, or raw blue agave syrup

1/2 cup ice

LET'S BLEND!

1. Blend all ingredients in a high speed blender until smooth.

Chef Tips

If you are using fresh fruit, just add a few ice cubes to the blender to turn this into a frozen smoothie.

MANGO COLADA SMOOTHIE

The Ultimate Tropical Experience

MAKES 2 SERVINGS
TOTAL TIME: 30 MINUTES OR LESS
GLUTEN-FREE | SOY-FREE | NUT-FREE | OIL-FREE

STUFF YOU NEED

1 frozen banana

2 cups frozen mango chunks

1/2 to 1 cup coconut milk

1/2 cup orange juice

1 to 2 Tbsps honey or raw blue agave nectar (optional)

LET'S BLEND!

1. Blend all ingredients in a high speed blender until smooth.

Chef Tips

For a thicker and creamier milk, add a total of 3 cups instead of 4.

VANILLA CASHEW MILK

Utterly Delicious (Moooo)

MAKES 6 TO 8 SERVINGS
TOTAL TIME: 30 MINUTES OR LESS (IF NUTS HAVE BEEN SOAKED IN ADVANCE)
GLUTEN-FREE | SOY-FREE | OIL-FREE

STUFF YOU NEED

1 cup raw cashews, soaked, drained, and rinsed

4 cups of water

2 Tbsps pure maple syrup, honey, or raw blue agave nectar

1 tsp vanilla flavoring
See page 10 for the vanilla bean equivalent

LET'S COOK!

1. In a high speed blender, blend cashews, sweetener, and vanilla flavoring together with two cups of water. Blend until completely smooth.
2. Add the remaining two cups of water.
3. Pour into an airtight container and refrigerate before serving.
4. This milk will keep in the refrigerator for approximately 4 to 5 days.

Chef Tips

Adjust water for desired thickness. Plant-based milks kept in a sealed jar will last in the refrigerator for 4 to 5 days.

OAT MILK

Breakfast Cereal Turned Into a Beverage

MAKES 6 TO 8 SERVINGS
TOTAL TIME: 30 MINUTES OR LESS (IF NUTS HAVE BEEN SOAKED IN ADVANCE)
GLUTEN-FREE | SOY-FREE | OIL-FREE

STUFF YOU NEED

1 cup oats
Use gluten-free oats if needed

1/4 cup raw cashews, soaked, drained, and rinsed

3 to 4 cups water

Pinch of Himalayan pink salt or salt of your choice

1 tsp vanilla flavoring (optional)
See page 10 for the vanilla bean equivalent

2 Tbsps pure maple syrup, honey, or raw blue agave nectar (optional)

LET'S COOK

1. Blend all ingredients in a high speed blender until smooth.
2. Strain through a nut milk bag or cheesecloth.
3. Twist gently to squeeze milk out.
4. Pour into a glass jar with lid.
5. Refrigerate before serving.

Chef Tips

Adjust water for desired thickness. Plant-based milks kept in a sealed jar will last in the refrigerator for 4 to 5 days.

RICE MILK

Rice is Nice

MAKES 6 TO 8 SERVINGS
TOTAL TIME: 30 MINUTES OR LESS (IF RICE HAS BEEN COOKED IN ADVANCE)
GLUTEN-FREE | SOY-FREE | NUT-FREE | OIL-FREE

STUFF YOU NEED

1 cup brown rice, cooked

3 to 4 cups water

Pinch of Himalayan pink salt or salt of your choice

1 tsp vanilla flavoring (optional)
See page 10 for the vanilla bean equivalent

1 to 2 Tbsps pure maple syrup, honey, or raw blue agave nectar (optional)

LET'S COOK

1. Blend all in a high speed blender until smooth.
2. Strain through a nut milk bag or cheesecloth.
3. Twist gently to squeeze milk out.
4. Pour into a glass jar with lid.
5. Refrigerate before serving.

Index

Acknowledgements

This book was a passion project of a wonderful team of people who made my dream become reality. But none of this would have been possible without Jesus right by our sides. We hope and pray that these recipes will be a blessing to you, and life-changing, as much as they have been to us and many others.

PRESIDENT OF WILDWOOD HEALTH INSTITUTE
Vaughan Sparrow

PRESIDENT OF LIGHT
James Hartley

EXECUTIVE PROJECT MANAGER FORMER DIRECTOR OF WILDWOOD LIFESTYLE CENTER
Pierre Potgieter

PROJECT MANAGER DIRECTOR OF WILDWOOD MEDIA PRODUCTIONS
Jonathan Suero

EDITOR
Danique Tersmette

ASSISTANT EDITOR
Aileen Corrigan

GRAPHIC DESIGNER
Xavier Hazen

ASSISTANT GRAPHIC DESIGNER
Danique Tersmette

PHOTOGRAPHERS
Xavier Hazen, Jonathan Suero, Danique Tersmette, and Svetlana Christian (3ABN)

PHOTO EDITING
Xavier Hazen, Jonathan Suero, and Daniel Atwood

VIDEO PRODUCTION
Jonathan Suero and Danique Tersmette

RECIPES REVIEWED BY WILDWOOD LIFESTYLE CENTER NUTRITION COMMITTEE
Mary Fisher, Cristine Castillo, Raven White, and Pierre Potgieter

COOKBOOK GENEROUSLY UNDERWRITTEN BY
Dr. Tim M. Riesenberger, MD, and Vaughan Sparrow

SPECIAL THANKS TO
My husband Ron Lynch who is my right-hand man, not only in the kitchen, but in all things. I love you with all my heart.

My sister Christine Mahesh, who has been the taste tester of my recipes almost her entire life. Thank you for helping me be the chef that I am today.

My dear friends and family who have supported me throughout this amazing journey. You know who you are. Thank you.

THE TEAM
Jonathan Suero, Danique Tersmette, Xavier Hazen, and Daniel Atwood as part of Wildwood Media Productions, have all worked so hard on managing, editing, and designing this cookbook. I am also incredibly grateful for those team members who filmed and edited many of the videos that can be found on social media today. This book wouldn't have been possible without the heart and soul that all of you have put into this project.

GET YOUR
HEALTH BACK
Naturally
WE CAN
HELP!
Wildwood
HEALTH INSTITUTE
WILDWOODHEALTH.COM
(800)-634-9355